THE FAILURE
OF FAITH

THE FAILURE OF FAITH

FROM CALVARY
TO TOKYO

Muir Weissinger

FORUM EDITIONS

Martin Luther King said; *"If a man hasn't discovered something he will die for, he isn't fit to live."* It is a macabre search where the finding a reason for dying is the only justification for one's existence.

Mussolini, in his speech (Napoli, 24th of Oct. 1922) on the eve of his 'march on Rome' (in reality they drove there), spoke to his 'crowd' announcing that *"We have created our myth. The myth is a faith, a passion. It is not necessary for it to be a reality... our myth, our myth is the greatness of the nation!"*

Why are there no other 'living' things in the Christian Heaven? You would expect to find some of 'God's' other creatures – ants, mosquitoes, elephants, orang-utangs enjoying 'the peace that passeth all understanding!' The answer is fairly obvious – man wrote the book and insists on his exclusive privilege – his *droit d'entrée*.

First published in Great Britain in 1997
by Forum Editions, PO Box 2985,
London W11 2WP.

Design, artwork & typesetting by John Cooper.
Film and halftone production by Wyvern 21, Bristol.
Printed in China.
Produced by Mandarin Offset Ltd.
Trade distribution – New Cavendish Books,
3 Denbigh Road, London W11 2SJ.

ISBN 1 872727 38 7 Paperback
ISBN 1 872727 53 0 Hardback

CONTENTS

AUTHOR'S NOTE

When the great philosophers of the third and fourth centuries BC produced their brilliant but divergent points of view on man, they tended, at least according to 20th-century 'standards', to use rather loose terminology. Scholars still argue over exactly what Aristotle or Plato meant by this or that word, but what the philosophers proposed for man and for society was reasonably clear despite this. Twentieth-century philosophy, on the other hand, seems to have retired into verbal analysis, trying to straighten out terminology. This has left the field of public morality open to the 'con men' of politics and religion. While Hitler's religion of race and Stalin's religion of economics murdered millions, philosophy continued to be the whetstone for words. In 'The Failure of Faith', I believe that it is better to use words imprecisely now, rather than to await the millennium of absolute precision.

I was a 'sometime' graduate of Columbia University which also defines my attendance record. The arguments expressed in this work were formed in my 'post graduate' years. This book might qualify as my unsubmitted thesis based on many years of reading and observation beyond the reach of Academe.

Muir Weissinger, Seville 1997

From Calvary to Tokyo.

INTRODUCTION

Man emerged as the dominant creature on Earth as a result of his ability to cooperate and communicate, as well as his knowledge-storing and tool-making abilities. When the available written-record begins a little over 5,000 years ago, religion, which is an integral aspect of what I will call the 'Faith Answer', was already a fundamental factor in social and intellectual life. And with the exception of brief historical pauses, it has continued to be a constant although shifting phenomenon in human history.

Priests of all Faiths have supplied 'answers' to man's evergreen questions. They have explained how the world was created, what makes the weather, what to do to improve the human race, how to end social conflict, and even how to distinguish saints from witches just by looking at the marks on their bodies.

On a more metaphysical level, they have presented formulae for getting to various heavens, for achieving immortality, for escaping pain and for perfectibility.

All these answers are derived from an *a priori* assumption that their sponsoring Faiths are necessarily right and absolutely true; so that, when in conflict with apparent observation, Faith simply transcends it. But, over this 5,000 year period the Faith Answers have been consistently wrong. Still, each new untried Faith Answer, each new solution or radical variant of an old one, can promise and no one can prove it false exactly because it is untried.

If man's ancient Faiths seem bizarre today, they usually become quite explicable (even 'normal') when returned to their historical contexts. Amid the martial materialism of the Roman Empire,[1] the emergence of Christianity[2] with its ideas of spiritual power, immortality and 'miraculism', was unimpeded by empirical science. No body of proven biological law could point out the absurdities of Mary's virgin birth; no chemist

[1] Chart points 1-11
[2] Ibid

9

could ridicule Jesus' water-into-wine experiment.

The successful establishment of Christianity[3], therefore, mainly depended on whether or not it was, at least at first, perceived as an alternative to the negative aspects of the system then in power. Its fantastic visions of graves bursting open and well-preserved Christians greeting the 'Second Coming' were of a piece with the claims of competing oriental mystery-cults. In other words, in its historical context, Christianity was not particularly weird.

Marxism's rise to power[4] began at a time when it was fashionable to believe that science was a universal clarifier and curer of earthly questions and problems. Marxism seemed to be the antidote to 19th-century capitalism, and calling it 'scientific' launched it into the superstitiously pro-science atmosphere of the time. Economics as a 'science' was too young to have a body of irrefutable law to contest Marx's claims. But now, except by some of today's left-over Marxists, economics is hardly regarded as a science. As practical experience mounted in the application of Marxist 'laws' to human society, the more fallacious they seemed, and the further away seemed the realization of those roseate cure-all promises. The apocalyptic miracles of Marxism – the disappearance of the state, the vanishing of crime and cruelty – seemed as likely as Christianity's water-into-wine, the resurrection of the dead or the Second Coming.

Christianity, as an antidote to the 'cruel but fair' materialism of Imperial Rome, and Marxism as an antidote to the impersonal and often cruel materialism of 19th-century capitalism, could have served as countervailances to the excesses of their times. But because their ideas were made permanent by the embalming fluid of a Faith System, they were no longer merely useful antidotes to the malaise of their time; they became absolutes, proof against changeful time itself. If they were now proposed for the first time it is unlikely that either Marxism or Christianity would be well received by todays intelligent *avant-garde*. Christianity's promises of miracles and immortality might possibly find a haven in Californian cult land. Marxism would prove even more difficult to root since its claim to being a science could not now be accepted, and state

[3] Chart points 4-8
[4] Chart points 56-60

ownership of everything would hardy look like a passage to the withering away of the state. Marxism and Christianity would arrive at a moment far off from their original historical contexts and so be inappropriate for enshrining.

The traditional religious Faiths have tended to retreat under the 'guns' of science and scepticism. Their congregations continue to diminish, while their 'priests' try to avoid any uncomfortable clash with dogma as they struggle to appeal to reason.

Meanwhile the fundamentalist versions of those same Faiths are filling their Mosques, Temples, and Churches. The fundamentalists are never saddled with ecclesiastical complexity. They leap over reason and appeal instead to unquestioning Faith, cradling their adepts in a cocoon of absolute certainty. For example, in 1994 Jewish and Islamic fundamentalists were both able to justify multiple murder in Palestine because they 'knew' they were right – each group owning a transcendent truth.

But what about the newer belief-systems competing for the Faith business in the latter part of the 20th-century? How do they perform within their current historical context? They express, almost universally, a reaction against both science and materialism. In that mood they suggest the similar protest of early Christianity; but now science, their sometime enemy, has developed too far for their magical-mystery-claims to go unchallenged. In relation to their historical context, the late 20th-century crop of Faith cults are more 'crack-pot'[5] and require a more total suspension of critical faculties than was previously necessary, simply because the body of countervailing knowledge and experience has increased exponentially.

But if the new Faith ideas of our times are relatively more fantastic than in other epochs, the techniques of conversion are firmly based on the latest laboratory findings of today's behavioural sciences. The publishing of details of a 'do-it-yourself' atomic bomb was fought by the United States government. But the details of 'do-it-yourself' Faith conversion are available to anyone. The prescribed diet, the interminable encounter sessions, often combined with very little sleep, are part of the deliberate disruption of an apprentice's personality defences.

[5] A sampling of contemporary cults reveals an extraordinary mishmash of weird ideas. The Worldwide Church of God believes that the Stone of Scone (under the throne in Westminster Abbey) was the stone from Bethel which David used as a pillow; Sun Myung Moon's Unification Church that 'God's Elect', 'the third Israel', will be the Korean people; the Divine Light that 'Advanced Saints can live on nectar alone'. For $5,000 Transcendental Meditation (T.M.) has offered a course that would 'let you walk through walls, become invisible – flying at will around rooms or anywhere'! The Way, Dr (a PhD from 'Pike's Peak University') Victor Paul Wierwille's 'Church', sums much of this up:... Move your lips, your tongue, your throat... rest your head back and breathe in deeply... What you speak is God's business.' (Quotation from T.M.'s and Wierwille's literature.)

11

Next, while the subject is bleary-eyed and weak, the Faith System's 'guru' and aides pour out their cocktail of nonsense couched in instant 'love talk', and another adept has been manufactured. Small wonder at finding the poisoned bodies of such adepts sprawled in Jonestown, Guyana, charcoaled in Koresh's, Waco Texas, Branch Davidian cult, and in Luc Jouret's 'up-market', international-Swiss 'Solar Temple' cult-shot, suffocated, and charred![6] These suicides may have lulled intelligent opinion into forgetting just how universally dangerous 'certainty' is in the hands of fanatics, because these cults sacrificed only their own.

But now the cult business may be changing, reaching out beyond the believers. On March 20th, 1995 Guru Shoko Asahara, of Aum Shinri Kyo (Supreme Truth) sent his 'missionaries' out to gas Tokyo's innocent morning commuters. Police later found ingredients to make enough deadly Sarin gas to kill 10,000,000 more. Meanwhile Shoko addressed his adepts, whose self-sacrificing contributions had purchased him a stretch Rolls-Royce limousine; "Disciples, the time to awaken and help me is upon you. I am waiting for you to help me with the salvation plan. Let us carry out the plan and greet death without regrets."

But the members of the Aum Shinri Kyo, Supreme Truth Sect did not commit suicide!

In June of 1995, a mentally disturbed man armed only with a screw-driver, who had nothing to do with the cult, hi-jacked a Japanese 747 Boeing jet on an internal flight. He had only to mention the name 'Aum Shinri Kyo' to be taken very seriously.

It's all there – 'Apocalypse Now', last warnings of earth-shattering events to come, together with a plan of sacrificial action, ambiented by an absolute fatalism based upon and rationalized by an absolute certainty.

Today the real threat to mankind comes not from natural catastrophe or even from man's technological carelessness. It comes from transcendental systems of justification, which, powered and condoned by their Faith cores, have inflicted otherwise inconceivable horrors on humanity, and continue to do so.

[6] In Jonestown, Guyana, on 18 November 1978, over 900 followers of the 'Reverend' Jim Jones died in an assisted mass-suicide, having imbibed Flavour-Aid laced with cyanide. On a tape, evidently recorded for posterity, Jones handles the doubts of a lady parishioner: 'Well, someday everybody dies...'
David Koresh's fiery confrontation with the FBI led to the suicide death of 80 members of his 'Branch Davidian' sect in February, 1993. At least 48 'adepts' of Luc Jouret's, 'Temple Solaire' committed suicide in October, 1994.

Later in the book there will be a discussion of how Faith Systems pretend to give meaning to death and how they awaken the paranoia that slumbers in most people.

Whatever provision the slow evolutionary process might eventually find to reconcile the social character of man with his destructive capabilities, the odds are that it will come too late.

By the imposition of an exponential growth rate of technological changes on earth, man has forced the issue. Man's emotional capabilities seem unable to deal with the products of his intellect. Like a child prodigy, capable of comprehending abstruse mathematics but unable to accept the necessity for the separation of his mother and father, man clings to his millennial love-affair with Faith Systems, while paradoxically unravelling the mechanics and composition of the universe.

Five thousand years of such wasteful and mistaken activities should perhaps be enough. But now that the technology of war and social control has the capacity to eliminate or destroy human life on earth as we know it, man cannot afford any further messianic solutions.

This may be man's last opportunity to defuse the intellectual and emotional mechanisms in himself and his society which make Faith Systems possible, for it is only in the service of such absolute answers that mankind will risk absolute extinction. It is Faith that will trigger the 'doomsday' weapon because only absolute Faith is capable of 'rationalizing' absolute destruction.

Since the first atomic bomb fell on Hiroshima a substantial body of world opinion has become increasingly preoccupied with the problem of whether man can survive his technological capacity to destroy himself. But while these 'headlines' continue to require the urgent attention of the world's statesmen, most people live with only occasional reference to this background fear, perhaps lulled excessively by the collapse of the Soviet Union.

Systematized Faiths impose their particular view of how man *should* be upon the reality of how man actually is. Their absolute certainty of rightness justifies their 'cradle to the grave' prescription for living, and even dying. But while Faith Systems are particularly insistent, this same tendency exists in all societies and even within much smaller social groupings. So what may be said about the abuses of Faith Sytems may be applied, albeit in a diluted form to all human organizations.

Some agnostics and even militant non-believers accept that 'faith' in general is an inevitable element in the human condition. One of the principal intentions of this book is to show that it is not; that, instead, it is more like an evolutionary tail in the human brain which should have 'dropped off' many years ago – something that is life-impeding at this stage of human evolution.

The book's first ten chapters examine how Faith Systems emerge, grow and establish their 'kingdom' over individuals. Chapters 11 and 12 are designed to help individuals erect a personal perspective, a vantage point for judging the exigencies of the society in which they live, to help distinguish between what society and custom 'legislate' as good and what may actually be good for themselves.

Beyond the supreme urgency of defusing the 'Faith Bomb', this book attempts to construct criteria for separating the 'transcendental' from the useful, challenging the *fiats* of Faith Systems and their left-overs. Once the sources of social and psychological rigidity in others, as well as in ourselves, are recognized and understood, these life-impeding forces may at last be removed, and individuals so liberated can begin to develop themselves in an exhilarating new context of freedom.

The 'sample' chart of Catholic Christianity that appears on page 174 is an integral part of the The Failure of Faith. Similar 'stock market' graphs could be traced for all major Faith Systems, but the Catholic Church was chosen because of its centralized power, known public image and longevity. All the points dated are discussed in the Appendix.

Chapter One
CONSTANT CHANGE

Man's hope of permanency and certainty are dashed by change, which is a paradoxical constant. The Faith Answer, because it is based on an absolute, necessarily conflicts with change. It needs a core of adepts who will 'stop at nothing' to spread and maintain it. Every Faith Answer that has become institutionalized has had these at its centre.
1. Paradox and the Faith Answer
2. Change and the Faith Answer
3. The Non-Moving Part
4. Perfection, Perspective and Faith

1. **Paradox and the Faith Answer**

All is paradox. The cosmos and the human being. As man speculates on his existence, on purpose, on ideas of right and wrong, he uncovers deep contradictions. And where he had hoped to find absolute values he encounters relative ones. Human beings search for an end to searching and that end can only be an unchanging absolute, something immortal, which is capable of surviving the complexity and change surrounding mankind. Once found, that 'absolute', that God or Faith Answer, is enshrined by its 'clergy' and protected, extended, and fought for by an army of messianic followers.

Wherever man looks, inner space, outer space, his own fifty centuries of recorded history, he will find, paradoxically, change as the only constant. From the pyramids to such ephemerals as Lenin's tomb, history is littered with droppings of bygone and present-day cults. One Faith Answer succeeds another, one great all-encompassing certainty is dethroned by the next. People give up their lives in worship; individuals are exhorted to 'find' themselves in the prevailing truths; the unwilling are excommunicated.

Most people would agree that they are not perfect. They

know that society is not perfect; an unsung guilt slumbers beneath the universal consciousness, awaiting definition and 'cure'. It could be a version of 'original sin' and Divine Forgiveness, or it could be Hitler's assault on the Jews in the march toward the millennium of racial perfection.

It is the Faith Answer that conceals the paradox marshalling and channelling human paranoia into social actions that seem inexplicable or absurd to later times: without a justifying Faith Answer the Jihads, crucifixions, pogroms, ritual castrations, Inquisitions, purge trials, 'liberation' armies, great causes of all sorts, fall into their disastrous perspectives. Surrounded now by insoluble contradictions once concealed by Faith the traveller finds himself a stranger in a strange land.

The real world *is* the 'strange land' of paradox, unsolved contradictions and flux, where there are only questions, no absolute answers. In this land man's millennial solutions to uncertainty are all empty and absurd; his worship of trees, war gods and virginity are as ridiculous as his religions of race and economy. But with the unveiling of the real world, the traveller, despite his immediate disillusionment and disappointment, may come to tolerate the paradox and apply its freeing values to his own existence. The acknowledgement of paradox means the unmasking of 'absolutes', the abandonment of unreal rigidities and the opening of a space into which the individual may expand.

The Faith Answer is opposed to change, to subjective individual values and unfettered speculation. As long as it imposes its super-truth, its transcendental reality, upon individuals, their existence will be diminished by its exigencies. History, as we will see, shows us the wasteful process of Faith Answers battling one another (as well as their waxing, waning and replacement) and the vapidity of their sacred claims and promises.

Faith answers that are far from political power, far from forcing both believers and non-believers into their Faith frame, are only oblique threats to those outside their discipline.

A Zen painting, a Haiku poem, or the repetition of a meditational word may lead an adept on toward an aspecific comprehension of the 'ineffable', the 'one and the many', 'universal forces'; but it will seldom lead to co-ordinated socio-political activism. Such believers who do not forcibly proselytize, and who choose to spend their lives praying or contemplating, stand outside the mainstream of systematized Faith.

There are, all over the world, millions of 'semi-believers' in Faiths or Faith Answers that are either growing toward power, are in power or whose power has faded. Even though the semi-believers would probably be unwilling to give or take life for their 'semi-beliefs, their personal lives are still, often deeply, influenced by the effects of religious training. Militant atheists, agnostics and cynics, under stress, frequently regress to their primal religious conditioning. Feelings of guilt persist in otherwise 'liberated' Catholics, sexuality may be disturbed by puritanical 'hand-me-downs'; automatic distaste for certain races, economic classes, for the 'low born' (as in India) can usually be traced to early religious training, and is responsible for much unconscious tension and otherwise inexplicable reflexive behaviour.

Such semi-believers make up the largest part of all those who 'believe'. They are, on account of the very tepidity of their beliefs, the ones best capable of re-assessing the value and validity of their Faith Answer. Zealots, who would overlook and excuse otherwise apparent shortcomings of their Faith, are, almost always, beyond the reach of fundamental questioning. Their minds are tight-closed about their Faith. Only time and events may weigh sufficiently to disabuse a zealot of his absolute belief. Such an adept, after years of genuflection, is loath to admit to wasted time, and so the damaging relationship – the misbegotten marriage – often continues to the tomb.

But the semi-believer has not the personal investment of the zealot in a Faith Answer and his diminished belief may permit a partially open mind, even while he mouths the jargon of Faith. In the struggle for power there are seldom enough true adepts to acquire control by themselves; they need the support of the infantry, the 'half-convinced'. When power is finally obtained, it is usually maintained by the acquiescence of the semi-believers. Those readers who feel themselves to be in this category should remember that they are an essential part of the 'background count' of every Faith Answer; that their lukewarm support, their lip service, is vital to institutionalized Faith.

Most Faiths are searching for control of, or influence over power in their society and, therefore, frequently seek to reinforce themselves by using the rationale of a Faith Belief System. It is from the junction of Faith and political power that the most complete social control of individuals results. The particular oppressiveness of that control originates in the transcendent objectives of the Faith Belief, its special relationship to 'truth' and the rigidity of its inner doctrinal core.

The characteristics of beliefs which oppress, or have such potential, are listed below. When a Faith Answer is subsequently discussed, it is one which answers 'yes' to all ten questions .

(1) Is there a codified body of correct beliefs?
(2) Is there a socio-political enforcement of belief?
(3) Are there clear insignia to show participation or acquiescence?
(4) Are adepts willing to give or take life for the cause?
(5) Are there expressed or tacit sumptuary restrictions or requirements?
(6) Is there intolerance of other ideas or beliefs?
(7) Is there a surpassing goal toward which adepts work?
(8) Is there an 'enemy'?
(9) Is there a sense of elitism in the initiated core of adepts?
(10) Do the adepts believe that the heart of their faith is eternal?

Any group or individual answering 'yes' to all ten questions is a fully-fledged believer in a Faith Answer. These ten characteristics of a Faith Answer apply to all politically-enshrined Faith systems when they are at the **height** of their power. Before they become fully established they may conceal some part of their aggressiveness and, when they lose, or suffer diminished power, their relative mildness derives only from their incapacity to enforce their will.

2. Change and the Faith Answer

If all existence is in flux, then to the extent that societies and individuals attempt to erect 'fixed stars' of reference, they will fail. Thus the failure of a Faith System is prefigured in the absolutes that form the very base of its structure. Astronomy now knows that there are no fixed stars; only stars which, because of man's tiny lifespan, seem not to move. The Faith Answer tries to stop motion and give man a feeling of eternal verity. Christianity almost managed to achieve this in the early medieval period. It had repossessed all the tools of intellectual activity – if you wanted knowledge you had to pay your Faith-dues at the local 'monastery'. Christianity might have held on for much longer but for the Crusades, which, ironically, brought the Christian knights errant into contact with other ways and Faiths, and damaged the closed system.[1]

Stalin understood this same danger when he sent returning prisoners-of-war off to concentration camps, rather than allow them to spread stories of other lands and life styles. The South African Afrikaner-dominated government resisted television in the country long after it was technically possible because they feared its Pandora's box effect on the minds of the black people they had isolated for so long.

In the past, one way of apparently bringing about a major change was the dethronement of one Faith Answer system by another, like the bloody termination of Tsarist Russian Orthodoxy by Leninist Marxism, or the Catholic conquest of Aztec Mexico. It has been like a struggle between rival embalmers who in their quest for business kill the Loved One. A new Faith Answer might offer some social utility at a given moment, but because of its insistence on being a 'fixed star' it attempts to embalm that moment forever and soon is out of sync with change.

If ideas for change were accepted without Faith lodestones, they could, in turn, yield to change as part of a general and

[1] Chart points 24-27

useful adaptive dynamic. To adopt an idea subject to obsolescence is to remove almost all danger of its enshrinement and consequently the possibility of its useless continuance. The cruelty of those who ride Faith Answers to positions of authority, and maintain themselves by policing the minds and bodies of their subjects, would be avoided by the drastic diminution of the power prize. The inevitable change of government built into democratic systems is a sensible attempt to enforce change by preventing the endless continuation of adherents to a particular view.

The prospect of impermanence is greatly feared and yet it is fundamental to all things; stasis or changelessness has only a theoretical existence. Man's poetry is saturated with impotent tears for his own impermanence.

If man could add enough zeros to his age and had a very low-geared time-lapse camera, he could see fabulous movies of granite mountains melting, species appearing and disappearing, as well as fellow men sermonizing on the permanence of their Faith Answers. In this perspective the absurdity of permanence is clear.

And now, with the technological developments of the 20th century,[2] there appears a new paradox: the adepts of some surpassing Faith Answer have the power to destroy all human life while trying to ensure the permanence of its own particular 'truth'. In the pursuit of the phantasmagoria of permanence, all may be lost.

However socially, economically or spiritually appropriate a Faith Answer may have seemed at the time of its emergence, by the time of its codification the ground of its *raison d'etre* will have changed. When it reaches and establishes its power it is moving against rather than with change. It will rewrite the past and claim to be the future. For contemporary 'reconstruction' of the past the visual media, film or television, and 'virtual reality' systems are especially effective. Events can be distorted, reconstructed or invented to fit the producer's 'worldview'. And those events become more believable to the viewers since they are made to feel that they are eye-witnesses to such concocted occurrences.

[2] Technological developments include atom, hydrogen, and neutron bombs, bacteriological warfare, etc., plus undoubtedly other more secret lethal devices.

The Faith Answer in power will remain as long as the show is convincing. Members of the audience do not, if the 'theatre ushers' can avoid it, leave (except by dying); it is intended that the audience never see any other show. Towards the close of the run one hears talk about better shows down the street, and there are quite a few comings and goings that the increasingly inattentive ushers do not catch. Suddenly, in the middle of the show, the house lights are turned up, the actors chased off the stage and the curtain rung down. An impresario steps to the microphone and asks the audience if it wasn't tired of that show anyway. Glancing about one sees the inattentive ushers gone and their replacements holding terrifying weapons facing the aisles. A couple of people who liked the old show admit it and are silenced in front of everyone. The rest, including the imported claque, applaud. The new ushers pass out a fresh programme. Soon the curtain opens and the show is on. Some of the old actors reappear in the audience and some of the audience is now on the stage. Costumes, lighting, sets, props, scripts, cast and director are different, but it is still a show and there in the theatre sits that embodiment of an actor's dream – an absolutely captive audience.

In the 'short' period of man's historical record change has been produced by the application of technology, by the results of the struggle of individuals to control each other and by the clash of social systems. The societal disequilibrium created by these potential change factors is softened, minimized or even eliminated for a while by the presence of a Faith Answer. Marxism for example, claims to have an answer to the 'chaos' of the social/individual clash. It claims to remove the contradictions upon which that clash is based. Medieval Christianity sanctified the *status quo* both socially and technologically. The Tokugawa Shogunate[3] of Japan restricted all foreign contacts for more than two hundred years, 'surgically' removing Christianity. Of course society-versus-individual clashes go on within Faith Answers, sometimes producing momentous world changes – Henry VIII[4] versus the papacy, Tito versus Soviet Marxism – but if the system remains strong enough it can hold back social and technological change.

[3] Tokugawa Shogunate (1603-1868). On 27 January 1614 Ieyasu began the serious suppression of Christianity. Before the mid-17th century it was almost totally eliminated, replete with massacres and martyrings.

[4] Chart point 39

Like a balloon squeezed in one quarter popping out in another, so individuals react to the pressures of a Faith Society. It is therefore vitally important for that society to provide tiring, energy-consuming activities for its 'congregation' – to absorb the extra pressure: Buddhists mumble 'magic' words interminably, Catholics recite their *Ave Marias,* Moslems – the Koran, and 'once upon a time' Marxists shouted slogans at struggle meetings.

Meanwhile, of course, great and basic but immensely slower changes are taking place in the cosmos, the solar system and man's immediate environment. The physical changes in the world and man's ideas rarely clash as they did when Leibnitz's philosophy's[5] – 'best of all possible world's'[6] – was abruptly made to seem ridiculous by the catastrophic eighteenth-century Lisbon earthquake.

An additional problem has appeared in the last 150 years: the *accelerating* rate of change. Man is increasingly faced with an impermanence of his own making. Highways, factories, towns and airports alter landscapes, change environments and disturb ecologies. The average travelling-speed on a transatlantic journey from London to New York 150 years ago would have been about thirty days; today it is four hours by supersonic jet, a ratio of 180:1. Balloonists in the early 19th-century reached air speeds of eighty kilometres an hour; astronauts have travelled at nearly forty-thousand kilometres an hour, a ratio of 500:1. Far greater 'destruction' ratios exist, for example, from gunpowder to a fifty-megaton hydrogen bomb. No one needs Wells' *Time Machine* to find change.

Druid tree-worship was cut back by Roman steel, the Aztec-Mayan and Inca religions were destroyed by steel, gunpowder and horses. Emperor-worship was blown up by the atomic bomb. Christianity was mortally damaged by opposing Heliocentricity and Evolution. 'Bluff it out' con men say: 'Who knows, you might get away with it!' Not that Christians who elevated scripture over science were Machiavellian con artists; they prayed that the challenge was wrong and hoped it would somehow go away if suppressed. And so they, like Stalin with Lysenko,[7] insisted on constructing science on a Faith base:

[5] Chart point 47

[6] Leibnitz's philosophical dictum that this world is the best possible world hardly made much sense in the face of the catastrophic Lisbon Earthquake of 1755. Four years later, Voltaire (see Chart No 47) satirized this doctrinaire optimism in *Candide* (1759).

[7] T. Lysenko (1898-1976) was a Soviet geneticist whose theories appealed to Stalin, since they implied the political possibility of perfecting society through a Marxist environment. If human genes responded positively to their environment, then the 'evils' of capitalism would be socially compounded, as would be the 'virtues' under communism. The scientific world outside the Soviet Union never took this seriously, but from 1935 to his official enshrinement in 1948 all contrary-minded geneticists in Russia were punished. After Stalin's death (9 March 1953), Lysenko and his theories progressively lost support, until with the fall of Khrushchev in 1964, he was removed from all political power.

'What's good for our Faith Answer must be true.' Unfortunately, in time those things eventually catch up with the best adepts, until their words and actions are all directed toward trying to hold back the dawn.

The purveyors of Faith have always opposed change once their Faith is established. They have fought it intellectually since the beginning of history. They have opposed it philosophically, they have opposed it politically, and they have suppressed science when it did not conform. Now they have to control the exponential rate of technological change, or else it might undermine their Faith-position.

3. The Non-Moving Part

Part of the Faith Answer's appeal derives from the chimerical desire, seemingly apparent in all ages, to find something that is capable of being without changing. But to exist is to change. Only nothingness is changeless. The supreme presumption of mankind has been to 'discover' an unchanging something(ness) within this 'multiverse' of flux, then worship it. Since all Faith Answers are implicitly or explicitly anchored to a denial of change, they are fundamentally false. Critics, however, do not fault Faith Answers in general for their unchanging absolutes, but for failure to bring about promised events. They do not see that all Faith Systems are doomed to fail simply because they are based on some unshakeable, unbreakable, 'non-negotiable' changeless absolute. The critics of Faith are critics of *a* Faith, not Faith in general. They point out a particular failure to 'deliver'– they cite chapter and verse of the details. After years of a Faith in power, the accumulated evidence of specific failure is not hard to find. But such critics have only helped open the way for the next Faith Answer with its backpack of other 'gods' and new solutions to the human dilemma.

Strip away the shell of rationalizing rhetoric and discover the non-moving part – it will be there somewhere. That part will be the essential magnet of aggressive and defensive sacrifice; it will be the operant core of the 'Answer's' mystique. If this part, which is the source of conflict with change, be removed, then the bundle of policies can be examined for positive suggestions without rhetoric and fantasy of Faith heat. It is for this non-moving part that they kill. For example, imagine the following:

Dragged before the Inquisition and questioned on Christian beliefs, the citizen praises everything Christ said:
"This was a great moral attitude, good stuff throughout –
neighbourliness, returning kindness for meanness, not
burying your talents... great stuff... a good way to live!
Just wish they hadn't put in that item about the resurrection... "

The Grand Inquisitor motions to two heavy-set Dominicans:
"How's the kindling situation?"
"Fine. We have a whole edition of *De Revolutionibus Orbium Coelestium*; it burns like crazy."
"We're truly sorry, but for the good of your immortal soul... at least you'll know that the heat's coming from Copernicus.[8] (To the Dominicans) Should be good for both their souls."

Christianity's non-moving central core is 'the resurrection of the body and the life of the world to come.' And so the Dominicans nod and prepare the faggots.

The idea of the non-moving part is a key to the group's power to draw in supporters willing to kill or be killed. It is the inmost nerve, the core of belief. To protect this from challenge and to cover the possession of 'absolute' truth, it is surrounded by a ring of 'paranoic' assertions. The faithful will enthusiastically discuss the outer rings of their belief. They enjoy it, like someone newly in love who finds ways to turn the conversation upon their absent lover. As the questioner bores inward toward the non-moving part, there are stronger assertions whose basis becomes less self-evident until the nerve is touched. There the discussion ends with aspersions on the soundness of the questioner's mental state, the producing of a book, or cut-off remarks such as 'Marx, Buddha, Christ are truth and if you don't see it there must be something wrong with you.' This truth is not an ordinary truth: it is a 'super truth'.

[8] Chart points 40, 44, 46

The geometry governing right-angles, circles, squares is fact; no armies crush resistance to its truthfulness, no firing squads, *fatwahs* or iron maidens enforce belief in them. People are free to agree or disagree with the geometrical text. No one worries except the teacher because everyone knows that these truths are demonstrable; that they are not dependent on faith.

So the Faith Answer is in possession of a 'super truth' which cavalierly transcends what appear to be the facts. It defines itself into logical existence and redefines opposing faiths and facts into a specially created garbage-can. The rhetoric is fantastic – everything is 'clear', 'obvious'. The only doubts seem to come from the possibly defective or recalcitrant mentality of the audience. Here we may find the reasons for non-compliance or opposition – stupidity, stubbornness, greediness, deafness, blindness, insanity and so on. And yet the same audience would probably agree on what a circle or triangle was – not even disputing the quantity of angular degrees said to be contained within them.

Why does the Faith Answer's 'super truth' need all this rhetoric, specialized vocabulary and screaming insistence? In the words of Hamlet's mother, 'The lady doth protest too much, methinks.' It is imposition and overlay; Nuremberg and May Day rallies, solemn high masses, hearts for Huitzilopochtli and Tezcatlipoca,[9] deafening music, endless speeches, like a paranoic shrieking out his certainty. But only the individual madman is confined to the asylum. Societal madness has the run of the earth.

Copernicus, Galileo, Newton, Darwin, Einstein, none of these gentlemen recruited armies or preached violence to put their truths across. Vital parts of the Newtonian System, which fortunately never found their way into any theology, were overthrown peacefully by the Michelson-Morley experiment.[10] No one found it necessary to shoot Albert Michelson, his partner Morley, Dr. Einstein, Lorentz, Minkowski, or anyone else who contributed to the Special and General Theories of Relativity. The only Faith Answer that impinged on these developments was the appearance of Nazism in the nineteen-thirties. Since relativity was developed by a Jew, Hitler took

[9] Huitzilopochtli and Tezcatlipoca are two of the four sons of the ancient Mexican gods of creation. Huitzilopochtli was the Aztec god of war and Tezcatlipoca was the god of darkness. Offering up one's heart to these deities was considered an honour.

[10] The Michelson-Morley experiment took place in 1887. It demonstrated that the Earth's motion was shown to have no effect on the velocity of light and laid part of the basis for Einstein's Theory of Relativity.

exception to it (Stalin didn't like it much either). And among the scientists who escaped Hitler or were thrown out of Germany were all those of Jewish origin who were working in the young field of High Energy Physics. This, fortunately, caused a critical delay in the Nazi development of the atomic bomb. It is a nice example of a Faith Answer's non-moving grid, anchored to an *idee fixe,* helping to destroy the system by its absolute rigidity.

4. Perfection, Perspective and Faith

Due to the continuous function of change and the fact that perfection cannot be improved upon or altered, change and perfection are mutually exclusive. Logically perfection, with its inherent stasis, is at odds with change; it is a word, a concept, rather than an attainable reality. Perfection is emotionally one of man's dearest fantasies and intellectually perhaps his favourite will-o'-the-wisp. But it cannot ever come to be and must be regretfully jettisoned.

Truth makes man and society emotionally and intellectually uncomfortable, but the shattering of man's illusions increases his physical and intellectual scope. *Truth is centrifugal while man's illusions are centripetal.* Ideas of perfection are confined, ideas of change limitless.

When the Catholic Church decreed a 'Crusade' against the Albigensian 'Heresy',[11] many people died but the species continued. The great melee of Faith Answers that made the Second World War possible finally produced a way of killing all human beings whatever their point of view, and there have been 'great' strides' in bacteriological and chemical warfare, pressing reasons for the rapid defusing, not just of the weapons, but of the Faith Answers that could rationalize their use. Even if there could be a perfect Faith Answer, it too would be obliterated and some 'other world' observer might call into question such a form of perfection which thought its worth sufficient to risk the destruction of the species.

Unfortunately, human beings lack the perspective of other-world observers. They are encamped first in themselves with

[11] Chart point 28

all their contradictory impulses and fears, then integrated, willingly or unwillingly, into groups. Even scientists, whose researches involve extreme scales of magnitude and time, do not seem to obtain much perspective for themselves.

Isaac Newton spent a great deal of his life absorbed in the Christian religion, the Joliot-Curies were Marxist, as was the great astronomer Harlow Shapley.[12]

The night sky should be more than a poetic lament to be shelved during sunlight. Its perspectives and flux are an ever present denial of man's invented absolutes.

Under Mao Tse-Tung a thousand former Chinese landowners could be spending their last living night in cells awaiting a morning execution. Their only crime a defined extent of ownership. The judge and the firing squad stroll under the stars. Their Faith Answer permits them to ignore the questions raised by the scale of the cosmos. Their education informs them that distances and orders of magnitude 'up there' are vast, but there are pressing things to do on earth: this group of landowners is about to die in the service of a man-concocted idea of perfection. A space visitor, speaking perfect Mandarin, arrives at the execution site:

"Tiny place you got here."

"China is a vast country."

"I just passed Betelgeuse. It's not the biggest star but it's four hundred million kilometres in diameter. I think your earth's about twelve thousand eight hundred, yet you say China's vast?"

"Well, that's referring to the earth's space. Would you mind moving your machine, we're quite busy here?"

"In a minute – why are all those other people who look like you tied up and on their knees?"

"They are about to die for crimes you wouldn't understand."

"You know all these people?"

"No, not one – and I'm glad of it – I'd hate to know such bad creatures."

"After you've killed them, you'll eat them?"

"Good gracious me, no! That would be barbaric."

12 Harlow Shapley (1885-1972) While increasing man's estimate of the size of his galaxy tenfold and consigning the solar system to a far-off-corner, Shapley treated Marxism as though it was an eternal answer to man's social questions.

"Then do you do this for sport?"

"Of course not, these are criminals."

"Ah, they've killed other people and so they're dangerous,"

"No, they haven't, but they are very dangerous. This is the part you wouldn't understand without extensive reading and indoctrination. I'm really sorry, I don't have time to explain Marx and Chairman Mao's adaptation of Marxist-Leninist principles to a predominantly peasant society, but we're already late..."

"According to my information, man is the only earth species that behaves like this... the others kill for food, sport, and in self-defence."

"We kill for principle, because man is the only rational animal on earth. These are landowners!"

"I don't think there is any reasoning with such a 'rational' animal – good-bye, landowners!"

"Good-bye, spaceman!"

As the spaceship rises the 'criminals' fall dead, victims of a well-rationalized certainty.

It seems obvious that constant change fatally damages the basis of earthbound ideas of perfection. But what is the significance to man of the micro and macro magnitudes which surround him? A *pi plus P meson*[13] system has a life of ten to the minus twenty-three seconds, the earth billions of years. On a far lesser scale, increasing the zoom magnification of a binocular microscope alters the object viewed: as the magnification increases, tiny unnoticed details gradually take over the field, filling it with their own landscapes only in turn to be broken down into new worlds with altered characteristics and perspectives. One moment something appears solidly itself, and the next something entirely different with no resemblance to what was seen before. That the last was contained in the first was true, but now it appears a separate entity. Its original appearance was only due to the observer's perspective.

So it is impossible for the space traveller, interrupting the 'subtle' work of the Maoist firing squad, to comprehend its urgent reasons for terminating the lives of the kneeling men.

[13] The meson, or the 'mesotron' as it was originally called, was discovered in the mid-1930s and announced by Neddermeyer, Anderson, Street and Stevenson in 1937. It is one of many elementary particles with very short half-lives.

The squad itself suffered from no 'poetic ambivalence' or inter-play with the paradoxical constant. It is the comfortable simplification of existence which man's reasoning devises that other-world observers might find so irrational. But it might be argued paradoxically that man, a thinking being, or at least a being that thinks he thinks, must for his peace of mind shut off questioning through belief in the stasis of some Faith Answer.

He lives less than one hundred effective years in an ever-changing cosmos where time and mass extend about him in perspectives of their contrary extremes. It is not surprising to find that man's so-called rationality, like a tentacle reaching outward from itself, recoils at the vast 'non-answer' world beyond, recoils and manufactures some certainty which his systematic thinking techniques can thankfully elaborate.

(A) The delights awaiting man's 'good' behaviour –
The pains of 'misconduct'.
(B) The punishments for 'deviation'.

Three Capuchins beheaded in the yeare 1648 by the Comand of Bafilides King of the Habeffines

Chapter Two
SOCIETY AND CONTROL

Society is shown to need a constantly changing audience to institutionalize its parade of Faith Answers and its stance of omniscience. What Society is really after is control of its members and the Faith Answer is its most effective ally.
1. The Mechanisms of Power
2. The Omniscient Society
3. Fallible Man Offered Perfection
4. Faith and the 5,000-Year-Old-Man

1. **The Mechanisms of the Faith Answer**

The group or society, although composed of individuals, is fundamentally different from them in construction, characteristics and capabilities. The more parts, the greater the difference between the parts and the whole. Quantity alters the quality of a group, changing its characteristics and capabilities as well as distancing the parts from the control centre and the formulation of its purposes. So the more supporters, the stronger the group, but the weaker the individual position in that group.

The capacity of a group to survive the death of its individual members creates an inherent difference between the whole and the parts. By replacing lost members a group can live on as a moving average, taking in and dropping people like the FIFO accounting system (first-in-first-out), or the changing inventory of a shop. A group's future is as certain as its ability to continue this replacement process. A Faith Answer group, with (inevitably) messianic aspirations to increase itself, contains within its rationale, transcendent promises to assure itself of an inflow of adepts. To the adepts their compact with the Faith System is usually based on the belief that 'service is perfect freedom', so that individuals are led to believe in an *identity of purpose* and an *absence of difference* between themselves and their group or society.

In fact, there are differences which are obscured or masked by the transcendent goals and 'holy' means. At the moment when adepts are required to give up their very existence for the preservation or extension of the Faith, this coincidence of purpose appears most complete.

And yet, paradoxically, it is at those moments of self-sacrifice that the differences between the Faith-Answer group and the individual within it are clearest. The group is concerned with its immortality; the individual expects to die, but all his reflexes fight for life. If the Faith Answer is to survive it is essential to reprogramme those reflexes, presenting individuals with group goals of such overriding importance that they would be willing to sacrifice themselves in exchange for participation in the group's importance and immortality.

The individual, his mind tired of searching, is susceptible to anything that promises certainty. He puts the telescope of the macrocosmos and microscope of the microcosmos to this 'faithful' Nelsonian blind eye,[1] because there everything is in motion, everything is in a dynamic relationship with everything else. Only change is a constant. That man can find a permanence to live and die for within this dynamically changing cosmos with its infinity of time-space perspectives, is suggestive of the Theatre of the Absurd.[2] And yet it is exactly this certainty and perfection that sells Faith.

When Khrushchev[3] revealed that many of Stalin's devils were simply personal enemies, usually falsely accused, who should be posthumously rehabilitated, and when the Catholic Church demoted saints[4] who had centuries of veneration behind them, they acknowledged error and tried to update Faith, but in both cases they bent the eternal belief-core, lessening the certainty. If Stalin as head of the 'proletarian dictatorship', with the approval of the Central Party Committee, performed these clearly reprehensible acts, then it is possible that serious crimes can be committed in the most perfect system, and that, in the other example, popes, supposedly infallible as to faith and morals, have venerated as saints a great

[1] Admiral Lord Horatio Nelson (1758-1805), during the Battle of Copenhagen (1801), was signalled by his superior officer, Sir Hyde Parker, to withdraw, but deliberately put a telescope to his blind eye so as not to see the signal.

[2] The Theatre of the Absurd acknowledges theatrically the 'absurdity' of the human condition. Through such playwrights as Ionesco, Genet, Beckett, Pinter and early Albee this often amusing attitude of supercilious despair enjoyed its maximum vogue in the 1950s and 1960s.

[3] Nikita Sergeyevich Khrushchev (1894-1971), First Secretary of the Communist Party of the USSR, on 24 February 1956, in a secret party session, attacked Stalinism and its results.

[4] In 1970, Pope Paul VI promulgated a new calendar of saints, excluding Saints Barbara, Catherine, Christopher and Ursula, among others, and 'demoting' for optional veneration Saints George, Januarius, Nicholas (Santa Claus) and Vitus, among others.

many persons who were just ordinary people and who, in some cases, may never have existed.

That society will grab at even weakly-developed Faith ideas to marshal its members has been shown throughout history. The Mormons of Utah and National Socialism (Nazism) are two recent examples. The Mormon angel Moroni appeared to Joseph Smith in an upstate New York forest glade and arranged for the printing of the Mormon Bible by simply producing the whole thing on solid gold plates. The reason none of these gold plates are around today is that Joseph Smith considered using them to pay his debts; but, of course, Moroni could not permit such a sacrilege and so sent them back up to Heaven. The Church of the Latter Day Saints founded upon, and still insisting upon, such evident nonsense, continues to be very prosperous, gaining converts at one of the highest rates for any Church in the world.

The Mormon Church may not yet have found a St. Augustine[5] to fix up its doctrine, nor does it yet have temporal power; but it should be remembered that Hitler's state was 'rationalized' by an astonishingly boring document of hate and energy, *Mein Kampf*, followed by the convoluted racial doggerel of Nazism's official philosopher, Alfred Rosenberg.[6] The Nazis had no Aquinas or Augustine either, but even so, they almost ruled the world.

The absurdity of the Faith has nothing to do with whether a society will accept it. All that matters is whether it can be used successfully by a group (or those who control the group) to control individuals. Later, when change, fashion, or military action have overthrown the belief-system, individuals begin to point openly to its absurdity.

Typical of all Faith Systems, Nazi science was only permitted to confirm its theology and so the grotesque pathology of the concentration camps started. Jews, Gypsies, and other 'inferior' races were studied for signs of racial deterioration; the 'proofs' were put in brine and sent for cataloguing and extended analysis to the famous Anthropological Institute at Berlin-Dahlem or to the University of Strasbourg. The awakening from Hitler's madhouse was a result of his military defeat, not

[5] Chart point 11
[6] Alfred Rosenberg (1893-1946) was executed in Nuremberg. His role in the Nazi hierarchy was greatly exaggerated. Albert Speer called Rosenberg's magnum opus, *The Myth of the Twentieth Century,* 'unreadable'.

through the disillusionment of his congregation. The naive consider the Hitlerian period a monadnock – a surprisingly sudden geological bump on an otherwise reasonable plain. But in the same period, within Stalin's highly elaborated and sophisticated Faith System, seven million or so Russian peasants died, directly or indirectly murdered, in the forced collectivization programme; there were purge trials, the Katyn Forest massacre of Polish officers and the Gulag Archipelago.

An elegant economic religion did away with millions, claiming that this was necessary for the 'solution of its economic problems'; while in Germany a muddled racial religion killed other millions 'solving its racial problems'; Even down to the approximate number of deaths, the two are the results of the two Faiths and disastrously similar. Instead of labelling his social undesirables 'Jewish', Stalin called them 'Kulaks' – which means 'tight-fisted', i.e. rich.

Society in its indiscriminate search for centripetal forces will cooperate in the maintenance of any established Faith Answer. Any attack upon one will appear to be an attack upon the other. The less committed can then be recruited to defend society from revolution or anarchy. If the challenge comes from another Faith Answer, there will be the reflexive defence of the conservatives, the old believers and those who have positions to lose. The attackers have the vital advantage of a fresh bundle of proposals in the Faith package, the little discussed but open positions of power, and their absolute certainty – a certainty that is not usually matched by the fervour of believers in a declining Faith. As the struggle continues and sharpens, as the capacity and tenacity of the assault becomes obvious, society 'observes' the relative strength and suddenly the mass of undecided are cheering the new Faith Answer.

❧

Suppose that instead of the usual replacement of one tried certainty by an untried certainty, society were faced with the replacement of certainty itself through a system of acknowledging only change, paradox and pragmatism. What difficulties would the challenger encounter?

All power would be lodged with the Faith System in control. Depending on its freshness and the totality of its embrace of the life of individuals, it would be easier or harder to remove. All Faith Answers attempt to control the flow of information in society. Access to the various public rostra is made a privilege, not a right. Education is one of the established Faith Answer's vital holdings. To decide what is to be taught is to possess a principal conditioning tool. To deprive dissident individuals of liberty is a power that is inherent in the 'logic' of a Faith Answer, which seldom tolerates fundamental criticism. Opposition is simply defined as a criminal act and therefore, like stealing, becomes a police matter. The denial of livelihood – excommunication – completes the basic Faith Answer Power System. This is a Damoclean sword hanging over every individual's act or utterance; it is a most efficient way of damping opposition at source.

Torturing and imprisonings are usually society's last resorts. They are more indications of fearfulness than strength. Excommunication in the high-power days of Catholicism meant the possibility of starving to death. No food, no fire, no water could be given anyone under this interdiction. But since the Church didn't own everything or have complete temporal power, powerful barons could occasionally resist or protect. The State ownership of everything that could permit the earning of income constitutes the ultimate refinement of Faith-Answer power. With this economic weapon, critics can be instantly reduced to beggary, and if that doesn't work, the rest of the arsenal is at the ready.

In their days of greatest power, the world's Faith Goliaths have seemed invincible, but have eventually been overcome by rivals and time. The rivals are usually not invading soldiers; they are pervading ideas. The challenged Faith Answer is maintained and prolonged by internal force frequently combined with the threat of external menace.

Here nationality, common fear, and Faith Answer meet in uncertain combination. Hitler used the Jews as an internal and external threat. The U.S.A. was an omnipresent 'paper tiger' while Mao Tse-Tung was consolidating Mao-Marxism in China. Long after the Duke of Brunswick's armies had ceased to threaten revolutionary France, the terror was justified by tales of 'brigands' and foreign armies, all threatening the Rousseauian 'Government of Reason'.[7]

The Faith Answer will use everything imaginable from secret police, unending propaganda, and even war to stay in power. Every Machiavellian resource may be tried, but it cannot succeed long unless it swallows its own message. It must believe in itself. Hitler, Mao and Robespierre could not have tolerated the assertion of selfish manipulation. An objective observer might view their political manoeuvres this way, but they believed that their means were sanctified by the great end. Similar means, when not so endowed, can be perceived even by the doers as questionable.

When Louis XVI chose to go to war as a way of saving the throne, the false note was obvious. He was an earnest believer in his Catholic God, but Rousseau's ideas[8] permeated the Court, touching him and undermining certainty. The Court no longer wholly believed in the old Catholic Monarchical Faith Answer, so its actions were contradictory and inconsistent, as was the advice given to the King. Apart from most of the early emigres who were inflexible monarchists, the cosmopolitan forces opposing the revolution were generally those which had already been somewhat penetrated by attacking Faith 'fashion' based on the ideas of Rousseau. It is not even enough to say 'We must kill or be killed', or 'They are out to steal our economic and social positions, therefore we must fight.' This might work well-enough for the threatened owners of those positions, but in order to recruit sufficient assistance, they must also sell the validity of their continued supremacy to numerous intelligent supporters. There is usually something vital missing from a sales pitch when the 'drummer'[9] himself is not sold on the product or has found no way to rationalize the retailing of a faulty product.

In 1943 Benito Mussolini's arrest outside the Royal Palace was easily managed. His bodyguards not only did not interfere but were left, forgotten by the conspirators, at the palace gates.

[7] Rousseau might have objected to having his name fundamentally associated with a government of 'Reason' that rationalized indiscriminate arrest and execution, called proudly the 'terror' in 1793-94. See also Chart point 47.

[8] Chart points 47, 51, 52

[9] American term for salesmen, especially 19th and early 20th century.

His chauffeur tamely took orders from others. No one sacrificed anything.

No such thing happened in 1944 to Hitler. All that was needed to end the massive July 20th coup was the bare sound of his voice over a poor telephone connection from Rastenberg. Generals and Field Marshals from all over Europe were soon dangling from meat hooks, biting on cyanide capsules or shooting themselves.

The difference between Hitler and Mussolini was that the former presented his people with a Faith Answer while the latter only offered a well-organized political show. Hitler added the non-moving part which was only eradicated by military obliteration. There is no doubt that even if Hitler had beaten the Russo-British-American coalition, the pseudo-science of his racial key would have eventually been deposed, but how long would it have taken? The Roman Catholic Church cooked up a batch of forgeries[10] by which the Emperor Constantine handed Rome to Pope Sylvester. It took hundreds of years before they were publicly disavowed. Meanwhile, life-times went by with the faithful believing the Church's lies.

In spite of the vastness and apparent invincibility of a politically-enthroned Faith Answer, it is never far from being 'just a pack of cards'. Its fatal enemy is doubt, which works like rust on its machinery so that from the outside it may look intact, but under strain it will break down.

When the First World War began, the Tsarist system was already penetrated by doubt. Military stresses, command incompetence, food shortages, fiscal pressures and the assault of a fresh Faith Answer wiped it out.

A climate of disbelief may be fatal to an entrenched Faith System, but that disbelief may be only a transitional phase pending the establishment of a new Faith Answer. The anarchists in Russia only helped create an intellectual and political vacuum into which Marxism could move. They saw the oppressive powers of the State and the relative helplessness of the individual. In a moment of simplistic reaction they attacked the 'State' and its functionaries. They did not carry their observation inward, behind the political power, to see

[10] Chart points 20, 24, 37.

what moved the State. The most oppressive systems are rationalized by extreme Faith fantasies. The strength of these bureaucracies and their enforcement mechanisms depends on the energizing delusory systems.

2. The Omniscient Society

In the cynic, the zealot or the half-doubting middle-of-the-roader is the deeply emplaced idea that society cannot survive without Faith Systems. The cynic, exempting himself, points to all those people 'out there' who could not live without a Faith Answer. 'They cannot live with only questions. They must have answers...' he says. 'Even false ones!'

But supposing that Egyptian society of the third millennium BC was deprived of the religious reason for building pyramids and embalming everything in sight; would life have collapsed or would social activity merely have been re-centred on less transcendent, everyday needs? The causality of natural phenomena such as the periodic flooding of the Nile and the movement of the sun across the sky would have to be answered by 'We do not know why', instead of instant explanations via the 'codified' supernatural.

As long as it is acceptable to answer the unknown with an explanation requiring some degree of the suspension of the critical faculties and the substitution of Faith, man will continue to be ignorant; and he will also celebrate that ignorance. The greatest, most solemn festivities designed by man may be unconsciously connected to the transubstantiation of ignorance into Faith – pontifical communion at Easter, the re-enactment of slavery in Egypt at Passover, the pilgrimage to Mecca and Ramadan, the journey to Lenin's Tomb and May Day, or Hitler's birthday and the Nazi *Parteitag.*

When the current Answer is seen to be failing and a fresh, untried one begins, there are new festivities, new fashions, a new 'lingo', new friends, new enemies and a new aesthetic. All of this is a cloak of ignorance, a societal legerdemain to turn intelligence from investigation to celebration.

Man has individually, but not societally, admitted ignorance.

Society always seems to have answers of some kind. Even if the answers are quite easily seen through as silly and inadequate, governments still try them on for size.

In May of 1980 a booklet was issued by the British Home Office called 'Protect and Survive'. Its stated purpose was to save people in the event of a nuclear attack. Apart from being of some slight value to persons living far from an explosion's epicentre, its main thrust is the maintenance of control by the central government. In order to ease transportation problems, people are told:

'We do not know what targets will be chosen... No part of the United Kingdom can be considered safe... Stay at home... If you move away... the authority in your new area will not help you... If you leave, your local authority may need to take your empty house for others to use so stay at home.'

Later on the government, evidently concerned about its files, asks people to 'attach an identification' to dead bodies and 'bury the body as soon as it is safe to go out, and mark the spot'. It would be difficult to imagine a more cretinous effort to manipulate people. But this is society pretending to wisdom, to helpfulness, attempting to disguise its true motive of tranquillizing for control purposes.

By implication the booklet claimed London to be as safe as the furthest part of Scotland. Why would a 50-megaton hydrogen bomb be delivered to a Scottish grouse moor except by mistake? These blatant examples of societal lying are only a visible tip of a much better-hidden and rationalized body of deceit. In Britain the Home Office brochure at least could be attacked (and was) by the press, e.g. the Manchester *Guardian*, August 4, 1980.

In the 19th-century a modest little book was published, reprinted since many times, called *Enquire Within Upon Everything*. It appears that the title has been the claim of the major Faith-Answer systems and their functionaries. This stance, and the assumed capacity to solve all questions, appeals strongly to most people. Life is more comfortable as an answer than as a question, and human beings have paid a consistently high price for their answers. There is no room for 'perhaps' in a Faith Answer. If it were tentative, it would not be able to defend itself against others which were positive.

3. Fallible Man Offered Perfection

Today's sceptic is frequently tomorrow's zealot if the Faith-purveyors can get to him. Saul, after being blinded by God, rejected his Jewish name, thenceforth using only its latinized equivalent – Paul. As Paul he went from Christian-hunter to super-missionary. Jesus went up to some hard-working fisher-men and said, 'Drop your nets and follow me, for I will make you fishers of men!' And they dropped their nets. Joseph Dzugaschvili reversed the process by entering a monastic school in minor orders and came out renamed Joseph Stalin. The claims for the curative powers of 19th-century snake-oil went upward in a continual auction until the list of maladies it would cure required microscopic print to put them all on the label. Any snake-oil which claimed less would have been uncompetitive. Faith Answers and curative powers for the 'faults' of man are similarly auctioned and labelled. The carry-ing of Mao's red talisman and the affective magic that was attributed to it easily trumps the old snake-oil vendors.

The Faith-Answer's success has come from society's con-stant search for a means to dominate its individual members and from the admitted fallibility of those individuals. Few dis-pute man's fallibility, and even fewer see the paradox that because man will agree so readily to any accusation of fallibil-ity, he can be taken over by Faith Answers purporting to be infallible; his painful questioning ends because his thinking is now directed into planning for some kind of certainty.

At one time, human beings, impelled by the necessities of life, killed and mutilated one another in the hope of propitiat-ing weather-, crop- and war-gods. They fought over grazing lands and fertile fields. Then came the gods of self-improve-ment and human beings assaulted one another in the names of truth, justice and love. In this second phase, human beings were no more changed than the weather or the crops. After all the mass imprisonings, the loss through Faith Answers of individual sense autonomy, the punishments, the building of shrines, the catechisms, the *kamikazes,* nothing had really changed. Like fashion which paints or does not paint stripes, shortens or lengthens or eliminates clothes, Faith Answers have performed cosmetic miracles so that changes appear to have taken place. But weathering removes the dyes and the same fallible desperate human being emerges again, ready for another dresser and another cosmetician.

Despite man-made certainties, such as the Second Coming, change continues creating greater and greater discrepancies between imagined truth and observable reality. The leap of Faith, once imperceptible to many, becomes olympic. As Christianity began to lose its battles with Heliocentricity and Evolution, for example, its published intellectual achievements declined in quality from Augustine and Aquinas to the Watch-Tower Press of the Jehovah's Witnesses. The same kind of intellectual shift, Marx to Meinhoff,[11] occurred in the Communist Faith Answer as it gradually became clear that egoism and inter-individual or group oppression do not at all vanish with the abolition of Capitalism.

Steal the security of certainty from him, and man must face the paradox, introducing 'perhaps' into his rhetoric, and doubt into his decisions. If rightness or wrongness cannot be known until the end, then all that man can know is the process and all that will remain will be the process. If man is to be changed, who will change him and who will provide the new grid or mould? The great experiments at changing man through Faith have all flopped. Even before the discovery and quantification of DNA,[12] the 20th Century was treated to the first effort at (man's) genetic engineering. Hitler was crude where others may be more subtle.

Society's business is control: *whatever levers it can find will be used.* If it can find a Faith Answer strong enough to persuade individuals to accept a semi-lobotomized existence as an antidote to their 'fallibility', it will employ it.

When the doors close behind you in the Old People's Home, in the prison, and in the 'mental' institution, the depersonalizing and substantive lobotomizing begin. For most of these

[11] Ulrike Marie Meinhoff (1934-1976), the real leader of the Baader-Meinhoff German-based terrorist group, probably wrote most of *The Concept of the Urban Guerrilla* (1971), frequently unclear and prone to make such silly statements as that the New Left stemmed historically and intellectually from the 'working class. That must have sounded strange to the New Left's guiding intellect, professor Herbert Marcuse.

[12] Deoxyribonucleic acid. In 1962 Francis Crick, Maurice Wilkins and John Watson received a Nobel prize for research into the DNA molecular structure. Since DNA is the means by which genetic inheritance is transmitted, this was the 20th century's first step toward the possibility of scientific genetic engineering.

institutions social control of their inmates is their first objective. And frequently, despite their public protestations to the contrary, it is their only one.

In raising beagles it has been discovered that good pack-work is done best by dogs of medium to moderately low intelligence led by a dog of slightly superior mentality. Breeders eliminate dogs showing too much brightness and individuality. No strong Faith-Answer society appreciates individuality in the ranks. For example, in Marxist rhetoric, 'individualism' is a dirty word. The philosopher-king is still one of Plato's more seductive political fantasies, but one wonders who elects the electors who search for and find this perfect personage. If man's universal fallibility is agreed, then who can decide properly upon what that specifically constitutes and the correctives to be applied? Perhaps a fallible person will have to decide this matter.

The snake-oil drummer announces the merits of his medicine: 'Try it! You'll like it!' he says.

People at the fair protest that this is exactly what the last drummer said. 'But that wasn't my snake-oil. The other guy was a fake.'

Someone yells, 'I tried yours, and it's no good... it made me sick.'

'It couldn't have been ours, maybe someone else's. Not possible. Ours is totally new!'

And the parade of drummers moves forever on through that town, the last leaving disillusionment and the next raising false hopes.

Because of death there is always a fresh audience for the Faith drummer. He calls out: 'This is new, this is different, and it is absolutely guaranteed!' But this is really the same old product repackaged; and the people buy it, every time.
The old people take their experience away with them as they fade and die – the new ones have no counterbalance to naivete, and so they are always the best customers.

The Faith Answer introduces an ideal of unchanging perfection and carries on *ad absurdum* until replaced, so that instead of following change comfortably, there is a constant succession of rigid facades which become more and more brittle as they resist their inevitable motion along the time scale. The building up and the collapsing of these quixotic structures has been the signal madness of human history.

4. Faith and the 5,000-Year-Old-Man

Human beings can love, the social entities can only reward and punish; and yet they must try to extract sacrificial love from individuals. This kind of love is not only a society's status symbol, but is brutally utilized for its aggrandizement.

A young Palestinian sits in his bomb packed vehicle with the detonator at the ready accelerating toward an Israeli bus. He knows that his reward for blowing himself up, along with whoever happened to be on the bus, will be an honoured spot in Mohammedan Paradise. He is young, untouched by cynicism, and totally persuaded of the rightness of his mission- a perfect candidate for Faith-exploitation. His Japanese spiritual 'ancestors', the *Kamikaze* pilots and *Kaiten* submariners were the apogee of Shinto sacrifice, the State's version of a sort of *Liebestod.* Packed in their planes and mini-submarines, those young men had no hope of survival – their vehicles were sealed warheads. They were persuaded to make the *ultimate sacrifice* for the love of an Emperor they could never know and the religion of a State he personified. The reminders of their sacrifice – sashes, caps, swords, letters and farewell poems are displayed at the Yasukuni Shrine[13] in Tokyo. That those midget submarines never sank a capital ship and that most of the Kamikaze pilots were futilely wasted is not written there.

History is loaded with examples of posthumous awards of 'tin and ribbon'. Joseph Addison,[14] in the play, *Cato,* summed up this genre when he had Cato say: 'I only regret I have but one life to lose for my country.' (Apparently Nathan Hale liked the script.)

[13] The Yasukuni Shrine in Tokyo is a Shinto sanctuary dedicated to those who have 'given' their lives for their country, mainly members of the armed forces.

[14] Joseph Addison (1672-1719), the English essayist, wrote the tragedy *Cato* (opened 13 April 1713) which was to a great extent a political vehicle with Roman Senators mouthing the liberal gospel of the English Whig Party. Nathan Hale (1756-1776) was captured and executed by the British forces as a spy. Before dying, he is reputed to have said, 'I only regret I have but one life to lose for my country.' The American 'Colonials' made him a hero and credited him, instead of Addison, with this super-patriotic speech.

As long as the social group is potentially immortal, it can expect to deal with an ever-changing mass of individuals. But what might happen if individuals stopped dying?

Imagine if it were possible for one man to have lived for five thousand years, observing the comings and goings of countless Faith Answers. How hard a convert he would be! He would have heard all the prayers, sermons and promises of the 'priesthoods', read the sacred literature, watched the wars, the regimentation and the ecstatic sacrifice of each new generation of adepts. To a 'cold caller' selling Faith at his front door he might excuse himself from signing up by explaining:

'If I joined, I would see your Faith die while I lived on – then the next belief to kill or die for would come along and I'd still be a registered believer in, say, tree spirits. My choice would eventually be to believe in everything or nothing. My creed would have to be, 'I believe in the power of the oak, the stream, the sun, the bull, and the crocodile. I would be a dialectical materialist hoping for Nirvana, a virulent atheist who believed in miracles and the Resurrection of the body. I would acknowledge the virtues of human sacrifice and castration, kill middle-class people, Jews, slaves, Gypsies, in fact, anyone who disputed my faith of the moment. I would be pronounced utterly mad.'

Society could probably deal with one 5,000-year-old-man. If he were not killed like Socrates for impiety, he would be cordoned off as a curiosity. After all, he would be one against many. But suppose the appearance of a deathless people: society would not have a constant moving-average to handle. The same people would be there. They wouldn't have died. Would *they* buy a continuous stream of Faith Answers calling for great individual sacrifice?

Society would no longer be able to deal with naive and inexperienced people, or those whose senility had eclipsed the value of their knowledge. No longer a sole repository for truth, or keeper of some fantastic eternal Faith flame, society would have to discover ways of justifying itself by being useful to individuals, by serving as an employee instead of an employer.

Invitations to forget yourself and merge with a Faith Answer.   **45**

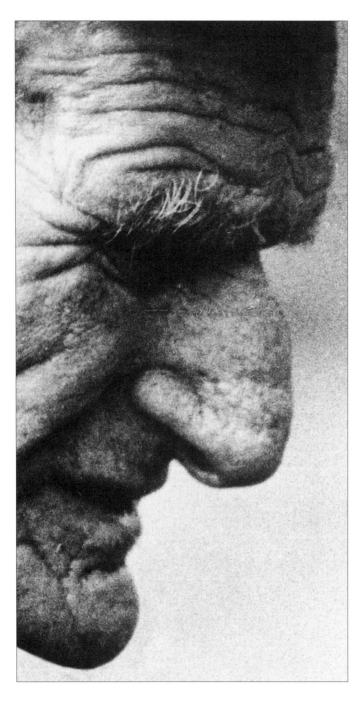

The 5,000 year old man who has watched Faith Fashions come and go,
and can no longer be convinced.

Chapter Three
THE DANGEROUS SENSUALIST

Sensualism – private pleasure – points away from absolutes toward variegation. It is the enemy of Faith Answers, which try to control it or invent mass substitutes.
1. Faith Systems and the Senses
2. A Way Out

Within a Faith-Answer society individuals generally work for a combination of reasons, often with very little reference to the Faith Answer of their time. In the 14th-century BC, an Aswan stonecutter, during Akhenaten's adventure into monotheism, probably had old embalming bills to pay and wanted extra corn (the money of that time) to start building his own house. He may have sung 'How beautiful, how beautiful' while he worked, but building monotheism with Aten[1] and the struggle with the Theban priests may not have been particularly important to him. The China of Mao's book tried hard not to let any person, even for one moment, forget their Great Answer. The Christian Church in its medieval glory forced vigorous exercises of piety on its members – the services of Matins, Lauds, Prime, Terce, Sext, None, Vespers and Compline, breviaries in hand, prayerbeads, crucifixes, genuflections and litanies; all of which make Mao's world seem quite lax. The Moslem Fundamentalist revival is at this writing exacting similar behaviour from its adepts- the attendance at prayers, the times for praying, the serious punishments meted out to 'black sheep', not to mention death threat *fatwahs* issued against 'recidivist' Moslems.

What the ordinary lay-person in the Christian/Mao/Moslem examples would want for himself, what his personal motivation might be, is hard to discover, because in the case of medieval Christianity reading and writing were restricted to the ruling party and, in the case of Maoist Society, access to

[1] The manifestation of Ra – the Egyptian sun god as the solar orb – was worshipped in the 14th century BC by the Pharaoh Akhenaten.

print depended on the ruling party's approval. Islamic 'political correctness' is enforced absolutely, where possible and by threats where 'Ayatollah' writ may be weaker. However, faithful though they may be, or seem to be to their society's Faith Answer, individuals may *also* be considerably motivated by sense pleasure. And most Faith Answers have gone to great lengths to pre-empt this.

Discrimination of taste in kinds of food, cut and colour of clothing, home decoration, sexual choice, music, reading, physical activity, all may endanger individual subservience to a monolith of societal Faith. For that reason the Faith Answers have tried (and frequently succeeded) in taking possession of individual sense-values and decreeing what is right for all the above individual choices. Even in the relatively permissive Western world, the growing of hair in the 1960s created a social explosion and the most astonishing variety of rationalizations for attempts to prohibit long hair in males. Case after case found its way into the courts and people were dismissed from schools and jobs. But the basic reason for the opposition was that it was seen as an emblem of social divergence.

The 'sensualist' has always been recognized as a societal enemy. Poor Epicurus, whose idea of sumptuous dining consisted of a bit of Cythian cheese, has been attacked as a high-living hedonist. The anti-Epicurean propaganda comes from his thesis that individual sense perception is the font of truth, and that neither the Gods nor the State need be involved in the personal sensation of pleasure. It would be hard for any social monolith to manipulate the holders of such ideas.

At the other extreme is the 'puritan', the abnegator of pleasure, the anti-sensualist. His disinterest in the variegation of choice allows him to give his whole being over to a Faith Answer, 'sacrificing' what he does not want, insouciant to others' pain. In the history of Faith-Answer societies there has always been a puritan founder accompanied soon by other puritans who serve and sacrifice at the vital beginnings. It will also be puritans who will preside over attempts at revival, and the sensualist who brings it down.

For example, Alexander VI,[2] father of extra-ecclesiastical children, high-liver, the most secular of popes, and Leo X,[3] patron of the arts in the grand tradition, were confronted by the revivalist ascetic monk Savonarola and by Martin Luther, respectively. Alexander had Savonarola burned and Leo more or less ignored Luther. The Church was at its most magnificent, but spiritually far from the days of the 11th-century when Pope Gregory[4], the Cluniac monk, arbitrated morality, punishing Kings and Emperors of the Western Christian world. Christianity had drifted a long way from the simple life of the founders and without these challenges might have faded away much sooner. A holy war is a powerful restorant for failing Faith. So the Reformation and Counter-Reformation, to the extent that physical and spiritual attacks were made upon the opposing adepts, were strong stimulants.

1. Faith Systems and the Senses

A group depends for its power on the discipline it imposes on its members and the quality and numbers of its adherents. In order to exact total obedience, it must promise to be the only way of attaining some surpassing goal. As a corollary, it must reduce the sensual choices of its adepts to those which focus on their participation in that Faith.

The pastoral peace and order of early medieval society has been much praised. People say that everyone had their identity, their function and that the social unit, the manor, was small enough to care for and about its members. Alienation was unknown and change was regarded with suspicion. This 'Garden of Eden' was achieved by reducing individuals to a 'catechism' life of firmly institutionalized functions whose parameters were limited by the struggle for subsistence amidst the entwined powers of priest and lord. Mobility hardly existed and the 'Tree of Knowledge' was owned by the Church. In this condition, people did not present much of a problem to the society; they remained weak, ignorant and respectful. To those proposing Faith Answers, this sort of deprivation can seem

[2] Chart point 37.
[3] Chart point 38.
[4] Chart point 24.

49

quite beautiful. Reduce man's range of sense perceptions, mix and-confuse these reporting faculties, and he becomes susceptible to suggestion. Therefore Faith Answers, to maintain themselves, must assault man's senses. They must deprive and substitute. The Christian Bible recommends plenty of fasting, abstention from sex and even sleepless nights – 'watching and fasting'. This is a popular recipe recommended by 20th-century cults.

Christ said, 'Take no thought for your life, what ye shall eat or what ye shall drink; nor yet for your body, what ye shall put on.'[5] Once again the principal of variegation of sense experience is seen opposed to the Faith Answer. Vanity is a sin, gluttony is a sin, fornication is a sin – the Catholic Church ran through every sense and found sin in them all. A nun would be all right smelling of church incense, but a personal bottle of Miss Dior would be cause for serious penance. In other words, a person follows the prescribed life-style of the Great Faith Answer at the expense of his individual sense-development, or is penalized for his independence.

To protect themselves from the exactions of Faith Answers, individuals must develop criteria for judging societal demands, and the criterion-base has to be their sense-perception system. All information enters through these discriminators and it is essential that they be free from taint. Someone who does not see properly, or hear well, whose sense of smell, taste, or touch, is seriously diminished, has a recognizable medical problem. The senses are not able to send accurate assessments of the outside world to the brain. When the senses transmit accurately, but the brain perverts and twists the information, there is an obvious mental problem. For example, if the sight of a red rose sends the viewer off into a killing spree, there may be nothing wrong with the seeing sense because it has accurately reported the red rose; but its meaning, its symbolic value, is involved with some serious psychosis. Freud found that any object could acquire sexual value simply by associative conditioning. Kraft-Ebbing[6] even notes a man whose walls were covered with stolen spectacles; he experienced intense sexual excitement in possessing eyeglasses.

[5] King James edition of New Testament, Matthew 6,25.
[6] Kraft-Ebbing *Psychopathia Sexualis* (1886).

These kinds of disturbances are clear and may need clinical assistance. But when a Faith Answer interferes with perception, no psychiatrists or group therapists are called. Suppression, alteration and the trained reaction to the messages of the senses are the objectives of all Faith Beliefs.

2. **A Way Out**

If someone is sending gas under your front door, it is up to the ears to hear and the nose to give you warning. The senses are protective sentinels and messengers of subjective existence. If they do not work well, existence is at risk. But the senses are not decision makers. They are more- or less- accurate reporters sending their observations to a distant command post. If the headquarters has been infiltrated, the most elaborate and pressing reports or observations may be disregarded. A team is sent out to check on possible border violations, but if one member, on instructions from his Faith Answer, defines a violation as something of which only the 'pagans' are capable, then he will blind himself to a whole invasion if it comes from the people of his own Faith. Early Christian adepts vied for martyrdom and the more agonizing it was the better, so the pain messages were altered by Faith into an ecstatic experience.

Unlike other animals, it is uniquely possible for humans to alter the significance of sense perception and reprogramme such natural rhythms as the eating-sleeping cycle through the use of language. This is done by literally going over the head of the senses. Other animals live outside 'word' rationale and cannot be seduced by the most inspired reasoning, acquiescence being secured directly through their sense perception of pleasure and pain.

The charge of sybaritic individualism should be expected from Faith Answer apologists. *There has not yet been a society that has officially approved of private pleasure.* Individual sense-pleasure is iconoclastic in its social effects and all societies have sought to define and control it. Even though the United States' Bill of Rights[7] contains a 'right to the pursuit of happiness' clause, there may have been as much or more American legis-

[7] The Bill of Rights became an integral part of the United States Constitution, 1791.

lation defining and controlling individual pleasure than in other 'liberal' societies. The banning of alcoholic beverages in the 1920s, and the constant see-saw fight with gambling, prostitution and subsequently marijuana are merely the more obvious examples. Until very recently, many of the states carried laws regulating what consenting adults, including husbands and wives, could do with each other in the privacy of their own homes.

It is also worth noting that in contemporary societies, where Faith Answers are not totally in control, the taxing power (amongst other laws) tends to discriminate against individual pleasure – theatre admissions, drinks, travel, cosmetics, etc. Naturally this is justified by saying that it is easier and fairer. But do not all Western societies have direct progressive income taxes based on an ability to pay? Who pays less taxes with the same income? The misanthropic miser or the people who eat and drink, go to the theatre, travel and so on? Obviously, the miser. He can sit at home saving his money while the others, in many cases poorer than he, pay taxes that he does not have to pay merely because they want to have a 'good time'. Where a Faith Answer is in control, the social thrust is to own and operate all possible pleasure outlets, diverting individual pleasure seekers, where possible, into Faith Answer activities redefined as happiness goals. Both the Nazi and Communist systems quickly took over the 'holiday-making' business and ruled on the content of entertainment.

Individual sense-pleasure, unless rigidly controlled and channelled, is a constant danger to the collectivistic centripetalism of a Faith-Answer society because, under such circumstances, value structures may well emerge entirely independent of those societally enshrined. An individual, having built such a value system, is far less manipulable by the centre. No group welcomes persons who are beyond its control and a Faith-Answer society does everything it can to keep out competing or different value, systems.

The established, officially-sanctioned, 'drinking' society of 'liberal' Western democracies attacked with fines and with jail-terms the smokers of hashish and marijuana. Laws were passed and learned books written on the evils of these soft drugs by people who had never tried them, people who were regular whisky or gin-and-tonic drinkers. United States presidential candidate Clinton admitted to 'lighting up' but, wary of 'crossing swords with the puritan-tinged anti-drug lobby, not to 'inhaling', which might have cost him the presidency.

Individuals who want to escape the unending exactions of Faith Answers must cleanse their sense-perception chain of reflex reactions conditioned by the presiding Faith System.

A Bishop inspecting a Spanish convent wrote: 'I came to a sweet smelling flower garden, perfumed by good reputation and sanctity.[8] The flowers were 130 nuns, who had never washed their feet, let alone their private parts. But with Faith, putridity equalled sanctity and the Bishop's reaction to his own olfactory reportage was changed from disgust to delight. Only by imposing its own scenario of existence on individuals can a Faith Answer 'prove' itself. But like the story of the Emperor's new clothes, it cannot permit the presence of active doubters, because its grand verities are imaginary. In its heyday of power it controls as much of individual sense input as possible through external regulation, as well as by behaviour conditioning through propaganda. Doubters are silenced so the converts see all things through 'Faith lenses', hear all things through 'Faith earphones', taste only the 'Faith diet', touch only through 'Faith gloves', smell with pleasure the filthy feet of 130 nuns, and no one asks embarrassing questions.

The way to individual sense-autonomy is paved by doubt. If whatever Faith Answer in power or seeking power is doubted, its exactions immediately become easy to question. Without the intrusive scenario of the Faith Answer, individuals could interpret for themselves the messages of their senses, deciding which they like and which they do not.

Any talk of amplifying the scope of one's senses will almost automatically bring on a second charge – egocentricity or selfish individualism. But selfishness, like virtue, is in the 'eye' of the beholder. It is a subjective judgement. One person viewing an action might call it 'selfish', another 'unselfish'.

[8] *Gatherings from Spain* (1846). Available in Everyman Edition.

No one who wishes to enlarge his own existence can proceed far without the help of other individuals. If this help is to have depth, it must have a foundation of mutuality, which means reciprocal giving. But reciprocal giving is not unselfishness; it is as much a trade as wheat for copper. There is no such thing as unselfishness, only the appearance of it relative to the observer. All human transactions are trades, whether or not consciously intended.

Below the level of conscious awareness there is an infinity of trades being consummated, of which the tracing of any single one is probably impossible. The appearance of unselfishness is created by a misunderstanding of the vast range of individual motivation in which giving a gift may be as satisfying to one person as burying money might be to another. Each action, i.e. the gifting or the burying, would be as positively reinforcing, relative to the doer, as the other, except that the gift-giver's 'selfishness' is likely to encourage reciprocity and further experience, while the burier's 'selfishness' leads directly to a dead end – a termination of that line of transactions.

Christian preachers, particularly, have scourged their congregations with charges of selfishness and self-centredness. But the endless dinners of Lucullus, the sybaritic luxury of Nero's Petronius or the owning of a 100 metre private yacht are no more egotistical displays than Jesus Christ's entry into martyrdom or the Guarde Rosse's decision to take Aldo Moro's life.[9]

So when someone accuses another person of being self-centred and egotistical, nothing important has been revealed other than the speaker's preferences, because neither the accused person nor the rest of Earth's human population can but follow a course of self-gratification (both conscious and subconscious).

In order to control a population whose individual criteria of pleasure, pain and happiness would be extremely diverse or variegated, a Faith Answer must interpose itself. Substituting its own value structure for supplying gratification (conscious and subconscious again) is the implicit task of any Faith Answer group. This is accomplished by convincing intelligent

[9] Aldo Moro was the former Prime Minister of Italy and the head of the Christian Democratic Party 'executed' by terrorists in 1978.

individuals that a Faith Answer is the possessor of a truth that is superior to anything those individuals might know or experience. *Hence what is real is what the believers believe to be real;* the rest live with a false appreciation of reality (the believers believe). The price of entry into this 'secure' world of certainty is unquestioning belief and consequent acquiescence in its hierarchy of rewards and punishments.

An individual accepting this compact can get on with the horrific business associated with systems of certainty. He will have no qualms, because 'the truth', 'the way', and 'the light', etc., have told him what to do. As an individual before 'conversion' he would never have considered washing his hands in a stranger's blood (as in the French Revolution), or blowing families to pieces (as in Northern Ireland), or the mass murderous 'ethnic cleansing' for a 'Greater Serbia' in Bosnia, the gassing of innocent metro riders in Tokyo for the sake of 'Supreme Truth', or any of the other acts that men of sufficient Faith do daily. These acts are labelled 'valiant', 'unselfish', and 'heroic' by the 'objective truths' they serve and so they seem, to the doer and all adepts in the audience. But they are merely the reflexive products of the new conditioning imposed by the Faith compact.

The Faith group in control assigns the highest values to sacrificial acts for its own benefit and, through adepts, supplies applause. The essence of the 'trick' is to persuade enough people that the so-called objective reality of the Faith Answer is superior to individual perceptions and subjective desiderata, and that it therefore has an absolute right to define good and evil and to reward and punish.

Through the mechanism of the institutionalized Faith compact, the centrifugal forces of individual sense-expansion are reduced and forced back towards the centre where they are 'disciplined' and redirected by the Faith Answer in power.

A Holy Banquet.
An Unholy Spread.

56

Chapter Four
FAITH: THE LOGIC OF PARANOIA

Faith answers elicit individuals' slumbering paranoia, using it to cement their absolutes and focusing it on their solutions to doubt and imperfection.

1. The Leap of Faith
2. The Faith Answer and Paranoia
3. Factors Producing Faith Answers

1. **The Leap of Faith**

Robespierre,[1] after he and the Hébertists had 'wiped out' Christianity in France, understood the value of belief: it would be a useful glue for his new society. So the 'Festival of the Supreme Being' was invented. But the source of the ritual was too rational. He openly based his idea on Rousseau, who says in *The Social Contract:* 'It is essential for the state that every citizen should have a religion to make him love his duties.'[2] The idea is obviously too 'logical'– *reductio ad absurdum* – to touch anyone seriously. In fact its absurdity may have helped precipitate Robespierre's downfall. The 'made-up' language of Esperanto may have collapsed for the same kind of reason – too much reason.

In Bengal, the Kali[3] adepts spent lifetimes of often violent acts to win a place in Kali's heart and a position in the hierarchy. Only a few rose far enough and lived long enough to be told the ultimate secret – that there is no Kali. Robespierre felt the rational need for shared belief and ritual, but unlike Kali, the machinery of his made-up Faith was no secret.

A revival preacher may himself know that he's a phoney, in it for the 'kicks' and the money; but he can still be a potent force for 'converting sinners'. It is essential that the 'sinners' do not know. The magic lies in not revealing how the trick is performed. No matter how useful it might be for a society to share a Faith, it cannot be produced without real belief.

[1] Maximilian Robespierre (1758-1794) used the cult of 'Reason', sponsored principally by Jacques Hébert (1757-1794), to attack establishment opposition. As soon as the Hébertists had served his purposes, he destroyed them, setting up the 'Cult of the Supreme Being', which was borrowed largely from Rousseau's *Savoyard Vicar.*

[2] Chart points 51, 52.

[3] Kali seems to belong to the late Epic Period of Hindu mythology. She is a manifestation of Siva's wife when she does the 'cosmic dance'. With a necklace of skulls and holding a blood-stained knife, her appearance is anything but peaceful. Nevertheless, she is supposed, paradoxically, to be able to perfect her followers. Death and destruction, which she also represents, seem to be perfect bedfellows of human fantasies and perfection. In another manifestation, she is Chamunda, 'Patron Saint' of those who give their lives for a cause.

'If there were no God, man would have invented him,' and perhaps he did, but not deliberately. 19th-century Marxism was messianic, and those who gave and took life for it would not have accepted it merely as a 'useful corrective' to 19th-century labour exploitation.

A society cannot enjoy both the truth and the fruits from the 'miracle of faith'. It cannot say: 'Let us agree to believe in what we know is not so, because it will get more work out of us and be a handy centripetal force, keeping our society strong, healthy, and happy.' The rational process cannot be used to create a Faith-belief; only to explain, codify and elaborate it. At the base of these sometimes intellectually impeccable structures is what the adepts tend to ignore – a tiny leap of Faith, that is, tiny in relation to these great structures.

Lying across Constable's field early in the morning, above the dawn mist, rises Salisbury Cathedral's spire. The flying buttresses and all but the very base gradually appear, except where the mist remains. One feels certain that such a beautiful, elegant and massive structure must, logically, touch the earth. Man's carefully elaborated Faith Answers, by their sheer intellectual weight would seem to be in contact with a ground reality. But a Faith Answer's core belief is only a wish-fulfilment fantasy arising from a fertile historical context. Its foundation is in the make-up of the human character, the power-play of groups and their non-conscious interaction to make that fantasy-obsession real.

St. Augustine,[4] blinded by his faith in Jesus Christ's miracles, disparaged similar miracles by Apollonius[5] of Tyana. Marx put down or ignored other economists; in fact, he put down almost everything which did not lead to the apotheosis of his economic faith. For example, why were people unwilling to kill for Keynes or Thorstein Veblen?[6]. Their theories were highly respected. In Keynes, the manipulation of the interest rate was a vital key, yet his adepts never considered slogans like 'Death or variable interest!' Yet for 'scientific Marxism' Stalin wiped out over seven million peasants during his early collectivization campaign in the 1930s, and Mao shot vast numbers of peasants and city people because they had more

[4] Chart point 11.

[5] Apollonius of Tyana 'flourished' in the mid-1st century AD. He was an ascetic Neo-Pythagorean philosopher who travelled widely in the East. He is credited with so many miracles – including bringing a corpse back to life in Rome – that many Christians have insisted he was apocryphal.

[6] John Maynard Keynes (1883-1946), first Baron of Tilton, laid especial emphasis on the manipulation of the interest rate in managing a full-employment, depressionless economy. Thorstein Veblen (1857-1929) lived in the United States in a period of the most exaggerated opulence and individual display. He analyzed the economics of this garish tendency critically, calling it 'conspicuous consumption'.

land or goods than some arbitrary norm. Why? Veblen and Keynes never asked their supporters for a suspension of their intellectual faculties. They laid out their theories without compulsion – they never asked for 'belief', they never asked anyone for *a priori* leaps of faith and never offered the devils-angels paranoia of a 'Great Answer'.

2. The Faith Answer and Paranoia

'The initial paranoid idea may be based on a simple situation, e.g. a sharp argument over a political view. This later may develop into a paranoid idea relating to a person or topic, which eventually, with time, dominates consciousness and becomes the central theme governing the individual's thoughts and behaviour. It is called an "over-valued idea" when there is a large affective (emotional) component associated, e.g. rage, jealousy, thwarted love.'[7]

The Faith Answer is the *Deus ex Machina* which ends the individual's uncomfortable questioning. The dormant paranoia that can be found in every human being is susceptible to stimulation and focusing. When this is done on a *mass scale*, it alters the norm so that the participating individuals cannot be 'certified'. On a small scale it is the principle of the lynch mob, and in the larger compass it is an Inquisition or Jihad, an Auschwitz or a Katyn.[8] Individuals after such terrible events say: 'Those people were crazy.' This avoids any understanding of the mechanism of social paranoia. They refuse to see that it was the group or society that was certifiable while the individuals remained sane.

It is precisely when man, concerned over his own fallibility, insists on finding infallibility in other men, a Pope, an Ayatollah, a prophet, a book, or an idea, and tries to institutionalize his 'discovery' into a system of perfection, that the mechanism of social paranoia is released.

Faith Answers and paranoia are linked. The paranoic 'knows' there is something terribly wrong. He is restless and confused. His mind resembles a wildly erratic searchlight looking for something specific on which to fix. People knowing him

[7] *Minski's Handbook of Psychiatry* Robert Priest & Gerald Woolfson (Heinmann 1978).

[8] In April 1943 German invaders of Russia discovered the remains of some 4,500 Polish officers in the Katyn Forest near Smolensk. They, and many more polish officers, were probably murdered so that there would be an upper echelon power vacuum in Poland, into which post-war Marxism could move. The absurd smokescreen of counter-recrimination by the Soviet prosecutor in the Nuremberg War Crimes' Trial, in which three inept witnesses were produced to accuse the Germans of the massacre, was worse than silence.

at this time might say he was disturbed, possibly dangerous. Then at last he finds something to fix onto; it becomes his explanation, no matter how fantastic, for everything he thinks is amiss. Suddenly his acquaintances find him calm, much better, his old disordered symptoms seem gone. He is calm because he 'knows' what is wrong, who the enemy is, where the power is and what he must do about it. Afterwards his landlady tells the police how considerate he was: 'Can you think of an explanation for these murders?' 'None, everyone liked him.' It is now easy to see that he is crazy. No rationalization, no matter how elegantly intricate or logically complete, is capable of convincing the judge of his sanity. However, if the court were to accept the premise in which the madman believed, the resultant acts might flow quite properly.

For example, a paranoic might believe that nurses are sexually more 'promiscuous' than other women, that sexual promiscuity is bad because it saps man's 'vital body fluids'. This must be stopped or men will be replaced as the dominant earth species by bugs which are capable of much faster generation, not being drained by promiscuity. In order to save the species, it is essential to punish and warn. Nurses should provide an appropriate example. Their death and sexual mutilation is therefore indicated. If one loves mankind and one believes that sexual promiscuity could seriously weaken the human species' reproductive power to the point that it would die out and be replaced by another more prolific species, then one's duty is clear. But, of course, so is society's: 'Remove that madman immediately!'

Groups participating in Faith Answers behave with equal paranoia. The universality of the mad premise protects them – no power left to lock them up. Frequently their only critics are rival groups who want to 'institutionalize' their own paranoia. Since the Russian Revolution, Christian sects and to some extent Zionism served as centres for disaffection within the Soviet Union.

The most potent opponents of the Shah in Iran were Moslem Fundamentalists, and to a much lesser extent a Moscow supported Communist Party. Caught between these Faith

Answers liberal democratic elements never had a chance. Not surprisingly, within a few weeks of the Shah's downfall the Fundamentalists were destroying the Iranian Communist Party.

If, in 15th-century Spain, the 'Grand Inquisitor' Torquemada[9] believed that Christ died on a cross to save mankind from sin, that three days after death he came back to life and flew up to heaven, you could hardly blame him for trying to rush heretic and heterodox people toward salvation – on racks, in Iron Maidens, on bonfires. After all, it was the immortal soul the Inquisition wished to save, the body was just a temporary thing.

Hitler 'knew'. Whether he 'believed' this is subject to current revisionist historical debate.

Hitler 'knew'* that the Jews and certain other 'races' were subhuman and responsible for the terrible state of things, and menaced the manifest destiny of the Great Aryan Race.

Stalin 'knew' that ultimate freedom, true democracy, and the perfect communism that would permit the withering away of the State were impeded by over seven million stubborn peasants, and by Leon Trotsky, Zinoviev and Kamenev[10] and thousands of others, so they had to die for everyone's benefit – even their own.

How about the Aztec priests ripping out the living heart from some healthy young warrior, temple priests castrating boys for the benefit of Diana of Ephesus, or monks and nuns whipping themselves? All acts, which if performed by individuals without the sanction of an established group belief, would be immediately recognized as insane – 'certifiably' insane.

Under the usual definitions of insanity society can never be mad because madness is 'outside' the social norm; it remains immune. The individual is always certifiable, not the society. This has terrible consequences: it means that isolated madness, the sacrifice of one or two nurses to save the race, is identifiable and regarded as dangerous. But if the group is large enough, any act is sane.

Some greater perspective on group activity is essential. The nurse-killer could only murder on a relatively small scale and would soon be put out of circulation. It takes a substantial group to do large-scale harm. In societal madness, the individ-

[9] Thomas de Torquemada (1420-1498), called 'The Scourge of Heresy', 'The Light of Spain', is the best known Spanish inquisitor, credited with up to 10,000 deaths.

[10] Grigori Eveevich Zinoviev (1883-1936) was a close associate of Lenin. Leo Borisovich Kamenev (1883-1936) was also one of the 'founders' of the Russian Revolution, being President of the Moscow Soviet in the key year, 1918. Both of these 'old guard' revolutionaries were executed by Stalin on 25 August 1936. As an addenda to this note, Leon Trotsky's assassination in Mexico (20 August 1940) lacked the cover-up of law. He was beyond Stalin's legal reach, so he had to be killed rather less circumspectly (died 21 August 1940).

uals tend to become cells, only carrying out a part of the total paranoia, sometimes so small as to be imperceptible to them. The telephone repairman called to fix a faulty Auschwitz telephone line, the secretary who typed up invoices for tubs of cyclon B granules, Hitler's vegetarian chef – none of these people, although important cells in the functioning social paranoia, necessarily felt in the least bit crazy. Even at the epicentre, Dr. Mengele worked hard exploring the pathology of 'subhumanism', having good days and bad, 'successes' and 'failures', doing his job. Later he was called the 'Mad Doctor of Auschwitz'. In fact, everyone who had anything to do with the racial policy and carrying it out later tended to be labelled crazy. For many it was disconcerting to discover how uncrazy Adolph Eichmann[11] was at his Jerusalem trial. The fallen Faith Answer, prostrate in front of a spectator world, is pronounced mad. The naive cannot see the cell-people who made it work as sane because then the matter is moved to a much higher level of investigation and complexity. Hitler's Faith-world would cease to be a comfortably dismissable monadnock.

Individuals – Hitlers, Stalins, Robespierres, Torquemadas – try to carry out what is to them the inevitable logic of their Faith Answer. It is in the certainty of righteousness that their 'evil' is contained.

That Great Faith Answers have succeeded one another throughout history means nothing to a new one. In the best paranoic tradition, history is simply rewritten to prove what the rationalizers require. New heroes and villains are found in the past, and some great future perfection projected which must be obtained by all means. That no such past ends have ever been obtained is unimportant; this one has to be because it is faultless. Now the plotters sit around their spirit stove and talk of means: 'You can't make an omelette without breaking eggs', 'the end justifies the means', 'he who is not with me is against me', and eventually the meeting breaks up late, each person tired but knowing what must be done and proud to be one of the doers. History is littered with means to unattained ends, from pyramids to kingsize gas-chambers.

Oliver Cromwell wrote, referring to the execution of

[11] Karl Adolf Eichmann (1906-1962), a middle-echelon executive in the coordination of Hitler's 'final solution' of the Jewish 'problem', was kidnapped by Israeli agents in Argentina and brought back to Jerusalem to be tried for war crimes. The world press played him up as a mad monster, 'Hitler's beast', for example. But his behaviour at the trial was more suggestive of a company director on trial for income tax evasion.

Charles I: 'It is easy to object to the glorious actings of God if we look too much upon the instruments...' But when Faith dies, only the instruments remain, so let us 'look... much upon the instruments.'

It seems that the longest-lived and most fervently believed in Faiths are the most impossible to accomplish: after all it is not possible to expect people to believe in and sacrifice for something already attained. The more impossible a goal the greater must be the Faith required to believe in it. The unattainable carrot, dangling eternally on the end of a stick, just out of range of the hungry donkey's mouth keeps him working the treadmill. Eventually the reward rots, or the donkey dies, and either a fresh carrot and/or a new donkey are required. It is essential that the donkey never gets enough carrot. A societal goal once achieved has no centripetal force and another has to be found. The United States' Space Programme, which had the specific objective of landing a man on the moon by 1970, was an important social sub-theme of the 1960s. It immediately lost its force upon attainment.

The touch of paranoia in each human being is the key to making a belief 'go critical'. Many beliefs have come and gone without becoming established. Some have been vitally useful to the *centralepolitique,* like the French revolutionary fear that the 'brigands are coming'. The machinery of the terror was greatly assisted by this strange paranoia. Curiously enough, in Russia, after the death of Boris Godunov, the arrival of various false Dimitris,[12] pretenders to the throne, and the total breakdown of government, there was no such 'great fear' even though the brigands did come and the 'time of troubles' continued for a whole generation. It was a real 'time of troubles'; there was no fantasy.

The South African government for decades whipped up white support for its *apartheid* policies by declaring that there was a '*swart gevaar*' (black danger) from the north of the country's borders, and a 'red peril' threat within from international communism. Since 1948 that government, until the dismantling of apartheid and the collapse of African communism, never lost a general election. During the 1994 South African

[12] After the death of Boris Godunov (1589-1605), there followed a period of anarchy, brigandage and pretenders to the throne. The worst of this 'time of troubles' was from 1606-1613).

elections White Rightists were still trying to play their 'red peril trump' card.

The flying-saucer cult is another social paranoia which has found no institutional home. On the surface it depends on a real possibility that some other planet might have a sufficiently developed science to send observers to Earth. But what do these observers want? They are the marionettes of the humans who 'see' them. That these extra-terrestrial beings with such an advanced technology should be so silly as to spend their visits to our planet 'buzzing' pilots and scaring farmers and out-of-the-way motorists is patently ridiculous. But there is still a substantial body of literature on the subject. One prestigious paper in Spain, the *ABC*, devoted a regular section to *'Ovnis en Andalucia'* – UFOs in Andalucia. Judging by the number of night 'sightings', the countryside should have been 'bright with the lights of UFOs.'

A part of the great success of the film *Close Encounters of the Third Kind* was that it presented a realization of this fairly generalized wish-fulfilment fantasy.

Having found no sufficiently charismatic guru, and perhaps dimmed by the real exploits of scientific space exploration, the Flying Saucer movement may be condemned to remaining a relatively harmless social paranoia.

3. Factors Producing Faith Answers

The real if paradoxical pleasure that is derived from the practice of masochism is probably experienced by many people who enter the physical and intellectual discipline of the Faith Answer world. The prostitute whose job was whipping a French Minister of War thought him 'very weird'. Oscar Wilde, at the height of his fame, spoke longingly of debasement, and got his wish. The incomparable haughty snob, Proust's Baron de Charlus, is discovered in a Parisian punishment parlour demanding more pain. As late as the Second World War, Jehovah's Witnesses were even asking Nazi whipmasters for a few more lashes, so happy were they to be beaten for their beliefs! These masochists are not so strange, nor are the paranoics; this is only part of the peculiar and contradictory nature of man which he must try to balance.

A singer, actress, writer, a political leader, anyone who becomes successful with crowds at a certain point, may be carried on far beyond applause to a 'mad' peak of godlike worship. It is up to the new 'people's choice' to find a balance inside himself or herself or be destroyed. All the elements of all the psychoses which man points to as madness are lurking inside himself, and can be induced environmentally or chemically. But perhaps for now, for today, they remain in a reasonable balance. All that is needed to summon these dybbuks[13] into action is some appealing Faith Answer and the weapons are in the hand; the once apparently balanced person is suddenly thrilled to live under what might objectively appear to be a virulently masochistic discipline.

So-called normal man reads of the Baron de Charlus, the Marquis de Sade, the 'mad' Goebbels, the 'beast' of Belsen, the massacre at Mylai, the mass suicide in Guyana, the summary British execution of German submariners in the First World War, the murderous Serbian 'ethnic cleansing' in Bosnia... and shudders: 'Crazy people, how could they do it?' The so-called normal man has not received his invitation to participate but when he does, he goes. His sleeping paranoia awakened, he marches off to monotonous music and idiotic sloganeering, ready to kill or to be killed for whatever 'it' is. Of course, if the right combination isn't found to move him, he can become a man of principle. Unfortunately, the principle enunciated is not, 'I won't fight period,' but really, 'I won't fight this one.' Such an apparently 'holy' pacifist objector to American intervention in Vietnam as Ulrike Meinhoff[14] was later to be found toting automatic weapons around the world in support of her band's own 'enthusiasm'.

A normal man, driving past a State mental institution may think how well 'trouble' is confined there. Strangely enough, none of the people in the professional enclosure would be capable of organizing mass subjugation and destruction. Whatever the worst criminal lunatic could do to society would be nothing compared to what one carefully chosen 'normal'

[13] Dybbuks are, in Jewish magical lore, spirits of the dead which can take over bodies of the living. Exorcising them is very difficult and requires the most powerful of Rabbis.

[14] See Chapter 2, Footnote 11.

man managed over Hiroshima. Parenthetically, it seems strange that the fatal force of the atomic bomb could not have been equally well demonstrated in Tokyo Bay instead of over a densely populated area killing over 80,000 people. But at that time the civilized world was teaching those 'crazies' a lesson. However, the other side suffered from the extraordinary delusion that they were the normal ones and their opponents were insane.

It is so much easier to avoid the mirror by insisting on madness as a prime factor in world horrors. What man does to man in the name of Faith Answers is not beyond the capability of the nice, friendly salt-borrowers next door. Very few madmen, except through inheritance, have become national leaders. But because of man's refusal to face himself, it is simpler to call them deranged than deal with the difficult implications of their normality. Then it seems that it is the normal man, driving past an asylum for the criminally insane, so relieved to see the guards on duty, who is the dangerous one. Knowing he is defined as normal and himself defining normal such as he, he steers on without questioning.

Both the tone and content of Hitler's speeches incited action. As his audience listened their adrenal secretions must have been at flood level, if judged only by the *'heiling'*, screaming and applause. Raised to such a peak of emotion, the crowd was provided with an outlet – through a Faith Answer which lifted all societal inhibitions in the direction of its specialized violence. It is ridiculous to assume that all the people at the great Nuremberg Rally were unbalanced because they approved of and fought for Hitler, even though some became concentration-camp guards, members of the 'final solution' team, or conducted pseudo-medical experiments on Jews and Gypsies. *The madness is in the Faith Answer, not in the individuals who follow it.* Relative to the context of their belief-structure as shared by millions of compatriots, they were as normal as the rest.

If individuals on both sides, perpetrating mutual horror and destruction can claim sanity and be right, the concept of sanity may be factored out of this equation. In the past, it was always customary for both sides to announce that God (or the gods) was personally interested in their side's victory. Therefore, in such cases, God can be let out of the matter. In the 20th-century, God, economy, race have all been invoked by battling nations. Any excuse seems to do as long as enough people can come to believe in it. But it has nothing to do with God, race or economics. It does have to do with the transaction by which the group 'plans' its immortality and the individual receives the comfort of certainty. If the group be increased sufficiently in size and becomes powerful enough, that certainty, no matter how objectively ridiculous it appears, can be 'defined' into truth and normality. From the Faith Answer's own super-truth flows its absolute rightness and certainty, as well as the logic of its messianic expansion. The group-individual 'devil's bargain' has rationalized both world wars and a severe diminution of individual sense autonomy. The Communist Party denied the validity of all wars except their wars – defined as wars of people's liberation. Medieval Catholicism did the same, calling them Crusades, while the followers of Islam call them Jihads.

As psychoanalysts or members of a therapy group bore inward toward the source of an individual's anxiety, so they come up against unconscious efforts to foil discovery of the truth, even though its finding could be crucial to a cure. It may be a damaging anxiety, but it is his – it is part of his psychophysiological image – and the patient instinctively resists its removal.

Normal man must become aware of the mechanisms inside himself and those of his social groupings which endanger his sense autonomy and his life. He is surrounded by disquieting paradoxes. He questions in order to end questioning and when his social group adopts an answer that will give him certainty, he contributes on that altar not only much of his sense autonomy, but also his life.

Despite the eventual subsidence of every one of these Faith Answers and its replacement by another, man has refused to learn from his history, always hoping that the latest Faith Answer will be *the* one. As long as he can be conned or con himself into leaps of Faith, society will continue presenting him with ridiculous new paradigms of human existence, new paths of absolute righteousness and ritual ways to behave. Yet the world turns, people eat, live, and are often happy without believing that God created the world in six days expressly for man, that the Earth is the centre of the cosmos, that Eve came from Adams rib etc. Cannot man also begin to see that human perfectability and changeless certainty are only 'willow-the-wisp' ideas foredoomed to impermanence in the real world of constant flux?

It is easy to object
to the glorious
actings of God,
if we look too
much upon the
instruments.

Bishop Ridley & Latimer Burnt at one Stake at Oxford

69

Church approved.
The truth of Earth's
place in the universe
was made to wait.

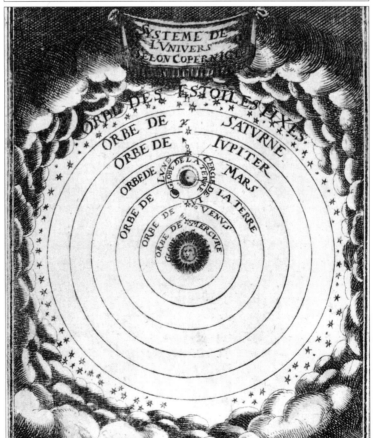

70

Chapter Five
FAITH, VARIEGATION, SCIENCE AND FASHION

Science, both theoretical and applied, without Faith Control is an engine of questioning and change and therefore potentially 'dangerous' to Faith Answers. Using mankind's social 'instinct', Faith Answers come to power like clothing fashions, but the changing of styles between Faiths is less congenial than clothing fashions – Faith Answers fight variegation in all aspects of life.
1. Science and Faith
2. Fashion

Major Faith Answers have superimposed on existence a pseudo-analytical grid to which reality is expected to conform.

The Ptolemaic geocentric system was unfortunately co-opted by the Church as appropriate to the Genesis creation story. Toward its end, the goecentric theory had been exquisitely refined, sporting fascinating rules for planetary motion in epicycles with retrograde movements, and the equant for some 'difficult to explain' cases. But it was absolutely wrong, and died hard because it 'proved' what the Church wanted to believe.

The opposite was true for Charles Darwin's Theory of Evolution.[1] It didn't fit with fundamentalist Faith, and for a long time was totally opposed by the Christian Establishment. *The Origin of the Species by Means of Natural Selection* was published in 1859, but the only Darwin given a biography in the 1890 edition of the *Encyclopaedia Brittanica* was Erasmus Darwin, his grandfather.

Stalin believed that his Socialist Russian society could be bettered by inheriting societally-acquired characteristics. A geneticist was found who agreed, and for more than twenty years Lysenko's theories were enshrined in Russia, while any

[1] Chart points 55, 56.

opposition was silenced, jailed or murdered.

When a Faith Answer takes over, everything must conform: science, aesthetics, the arts, clothing, housing – everything. The internal logic is perfect. If this is The Answer, it is the future; it is also the negation of the past except that which led to it. Thus, for a good Christian in the Middle-Ages, Epicurus would be anathema, but Aristotle one of the great pagans. From the sense of high mission to the details of its accomplishment, one moves from Aquinas to the Inquisition, and from Marx to the Gulag Archipelago, the fine points of doctrine costing anything from a squashed or frozen thumb to death.

Gradually the semi-private preferences of leaders appear. 'Socialist Realism' became the name of the art that party leaders liked, 'decadent' what they did not. Goebbel's famous museum of non-Aryan decadence featured everything interesting in pre-Nazi German culture. It was the last chance for thousands to see it before the boring Nazi cultural monolith took over completely.

Variegation is the enemy of the Faith Answer because it is a centrifugal force. It is an open insignia of individualism. The essence of a group is centripetalism. A group cannot deny its inherent quality of centripetality and remain a functioning association. In the late 19th-century Bakunin and friends used to enjoy interrupting political meetings and, if possible, preventing further deliberations. He and his fellow anarchists finally banded together into an organized political group whose meetings were so forcefully chaired by the founder himself that the paradox between theory and practice became obvious. When old-time supporters insisted on the anarchist right (rite) to interject complaints, they were thrown out. Of course, this 'organization' collapsed.

Variegation of choice in any society results in proliferation of interest which is always regarded by the believers as 'sinful'. When Nikita Khrushchev ordered a custom-made Italian silk suit, when the Thermidorians[2] abandoned puritanical Jacobin fashion, when the Crusaders adopted the luxuries of the East, it was a strong indication of a Faith Answer in decline. What would have happened, or what would it have meant, if Jesus

2 'Thermidoreans' refers to those involved in the overthrow of Robespierre on 27 July, 1794 and the often eccentric types who surfaced in the less-repressed post-Robespierre 'social' atmosphere.

Christ's Last Supper menu ran into fifteen courses; stuffed ortolans, wild ducks *en cocotte,* jugged hare, Damian, Thracian, and Rhodian wines? The faithful wanted to know that it was, in fact, a miserable dinner – he fed the five thousand[3] much better.

The founder of a religious organization was once asked by reporters how he squared his luxury trans-atlantic ship suite with his ideals. His answer: 'God always travels first class.' New Faith organizations chaired by high-living sensualists generally have a short life-expectancy.

1. **Science and Faith**

In the period following the Peloponnesian War, up to the 1st century BC, Hellenistic science burgeoned – mathematics, statics, hydraulics; even a steam-reaction engine was developed. And although oriental mystery-cults such as Isis, Osiris and Zoroaster were becoming more and more popular, they were not yet fully established. The moral disillusionment and the political confusion resulting from the collapse of belief in the Greek Polis (city-state), and consequently in its source of ethical values, allowed a period of doubt, of questioning. For a couple of hundred years, Plato, Aristotle, Epicurus, Zeno and Chryssipus (the Stoic), Pyrrho (the Sceptic), and Diogenes (the Cynic) preferred different ways of looking at man and his world, while science developed so far that its level was not equalled again until the time of Leonardo da Vinci.

From the 2nd-century BC onwards, the oriental mystery cults, as well as Neoplatonism and, most importantly, Christianity, increasingly combined to sit like a dead weight on science and non-religious speculation, an intellectual and material robbery of some sixteen hundred years of man's developmental possibilities.

The Renaissance, with its classical rather than Christian tones, began a cautious return to scientific speculation, but was closely watched and hampered by the Catholic Church. Galileo's support of the Copernican Heliocentric Theory brought him to the threshold of the Inquisition. A high

[3] Matthew 14, 13-21. Five loaves and two fish, with the appropriate blessing, fed five-thousand men, apparently to surfeit, because twelve baskets of uneaten food were gathered up. On another occasion seven loaves and a few small fish fed four thousand men, with seven extra baskets of left-over food (Matthew 16, 32-39). The total number of people benefitting from these two miracles should probably be doubled, because women and children were also fed, but no one counted them.

Ecclesiastic is supposed to have remarked of Galileo: 'Show him the instruments. He understands machinery.'

Hanging over the great Greek scientific achievements as well as the impressive societal speculations of Hellenic philosophy, were the oriental mystery-cults. Hellenic deities such as Ephesian Artemis and Dionysius were deeply penetrated by oriental influences. *The Golden Ass*, a Hellenistic novel by Apuleius, illustrates the dilemma. At first Rabelaisianly bawdy and hilariously absurd, it all ends up in a ceremony instructive (for scholars perhaps) but dull, a homage to the great goddess Isis through whose mystical powers the Golden Ass resumes human form. As the miracle of Faith restores the man's body, laughter ends and an uncomfortable irony emerges: the man in the ass's body was somehow far more human than the man of Faith returning to his own shape. As Faith enters, humour leaves. 'All encompassing' Faith Answers do not seem able to encompass laughter.

When the heavy curtain of Christian certainty finally closed the schools of Athens, terminating all non-Christian speculation,[4] individuals were sentenced to more than a thousand years of oppressive Christian nit-picking and for much of the period, a life lived on an increasingly primitive scale.

Faith systems, in accordance with their power, hamper, oppose or prevent intellectual activity that they cannot effectively 'guide'. Nor are they prepared to permit scientific discoveries that might interfere with their Faith Grid. They therefore seek to control science and with it man's extension of his senses.

Throughout the 20th-century, man's senses as well as his physical and intellectual capacities have been greatly extended. Micro-manipulation for hand motions of impossible delicacy, amplification devices for inaudible sounds, X-radiography for 'unseeable' light, industrial warning sniffers for undetectable smells, fast transportation as a substitute for feet, weight-lifting machinery for arms, computer banks for memory, all these things extend man's senses and his capacities. But there is no way to tell what a researcher might find out.

Both in his wars and his Faith Beliefs, man subjugates sci-

[4] Although the Roman Emperor, Theodosius 1 (AD 346-395) made life extremely difficult for non-Christians, it was Justinian (AD 483-562) who, in AD 529, put an end to the schools of Athens, and all but the most rigidly licensed 'establishment' Christian speculation.

74

ence and speculation. War and Faith Belief are usually connected, the latter justifying the former, often within the same belief system. Yet the final lasting fallout from a historical period are the decorations of its Faith Answers and the tools of its technology. The practical utilization of the wheel is far more important than the beliefs of the society that introduced it.

The coming of the Iron Age easily transcends the value to our time of the reigning Hittite gods of second millennium Anatolia. How important is it that Archimedes may have been an agnostic, Newton an enthusiastic Christian Bible scholar, Einstein a supporter of Left-leaning causes, or that the two sponsoring powers of the Atomic Age were capitalist? As time enforces a reduction in the relative importance of things once believed to be surpassingly essential, one finds, as in the retreating focus of the zoom-lens binocular-microscope, that very little of the original topography remains. The 'burning' differences between Paulicians, Gnostics, Arians, Hussites, Menscheviks, Albigensians, Trotskyites, Monophysites, Maoists, Pelagians, Stalinists, Diversionists, Deviationists of the right or left, Jehovah's Witnesses, Buddhists, Shi'ites, Sunis, Druids, even the Ra Horakty of Akhenaten and the Amun Ra of Thebes,[5] will all one day be melted into a catch-all called religion, mostly identifiable through the preservation of their temples. If, in three thousand years, Mao and Lenin's Tombs are still preserved along with the pyramid of Khufu (Cheops), the Buddhist caves of India, the Ka'ba in Mecca, the Parthenon and Chartres, then Communism might too have its relics. Hitler, in the middle of the Second World War, ordered his architect, Albert Speer, to continue work on his monumental Faith structures and gave him the necessary priority requisitions until the bombers came, destroying even the models. Nazism's relics may, in fact, be the concentration camp memorials.

The essential logic of the group, its power and potential immortality, tends to result in self-glorifying projects to which individuals contribute their lifetimes, suppressing personal dreams for the 'privilege' of 'getting high' on a group Answer. For example, it is possible to imagine a Faith employing the tal-

[5] The Paulicians, Gnostics, Arians, Hussites, Albigensians, Monophysites, Pelagians are all variants of Christianity, 'worthy' (at different periods in church history) of death. In the fallen Marxist world, Mensheviks, Maximilists, Trotsky-ites, Stalinists, Maoists, Diversionists, Deviationists of the Right and Left all can be worthy of censure or death. The struggle between the conservative priests of the Amun Ra of Thebes and the monotheistic preferences of the Pharaoh Akhenaten for the 'spirit' of the solar orb Ra-Horakty is illustrated by the changing of Tut-ankh*aten's* name to Tut-ankh-amun. Since Akhenaten's heir was not more than twenty when he died, reigning approximately eight years, the change of name was probably forced upon him.

ents of a Dr. Land for some 'defence' project, but certainly not for the development of the Polaroid Land Camera whose uses and pleasures would have been too individual. To take the first reaction-motor and use it to make some god's image turn round mysteriously or, two thousand and two hundred years later, to dump explosives on an enemy – these are what Faith Answers do with technology and great discoveries.

In 1942, a Jew is asked to stand at a counter and fill out a very long information form. By the time he has finished, the work of the Curies and Dr. Roentgen has had a Faith 'fruition'. The Jew has, unknowingly, been sterilized by an X-ray machine cunningly concealed behind the counter's panelling. Pavlov, working in and effectively creating the study of behaviourism, hoped his work would elucidate dark areas of human psycho-physiological response. His government sought few therapeutic uses for its people, but rather used Pavlov's theories to build Show Trial confessions leading to techniques of so-called 'brain washing', primarily for political rather than therapeutic purposes. Leonardo da Vinci's time was much divided between glorifying Roman Catholicism and sketching fantastic war gadgetry for the Florentine State. He wanted to fly; but, apart from his faulty aerodynamics, the bombs weren't ready! Bring an invention to the State, and it will be examined for its war power or control applications – without these potentials, enthusiasm will lapse.

So, what happened between 200 BC and Copernicus,[6] apart from the Imperial and tribal wars of expansion and contraction? Roman literature passed through its gala period, Horace, Virgil, Pliny, tailing off in the early sixth century AD with Boethius' *Consolations of Philosophy*. Painting followed a not dissimilar trajectory, being largely displaced by religious mosaics which, in turn, generally declined in quality after the 6th-century (until its 12th-century revival). Sculpture also turned to stolid, squat Christs and saints, disappearing almost completely in the Byzantine Empire principally because of sporadic religious prohibitions against representing the 'divine'. Architecture, too, declined after Justinian's rebuilding of the cathedral Hagia Sophia[7] (circa AD 560), taken over almost

[6] Chart point 40.
[7] Hagia Sophia—Holy Wisdom—is, despite damage and alterations, still standing as a museum in Istanbul (Constantinople) .

completely by Christian cult requirements.

'People things' like private and public baths, central heating, sewage disposal, public toilets, fire departments, theatre, non-religious literature, safe and rapid travel, innovative medical attention at treatment centres for the sick, and schools teaching other subjects than those specified by the Church, all disappeared totally in the West, while in the eastern Roman Empire only vestiges of these things remained. Still, when the Crusaders ravished Constantinople in AD 1204, those vestiges astonished the ignorant invading 'Christian' ruffians. Even as late as the 17th-century in France, at the time the leading European nation, Louis XIV found it necessary to post notices all over his new palace of Versailles forbidding nobles to urinate and defecate wherever they liked.

At this point, the what-ifs are tempting? What if, in the year 200 BC, religion had vanished from the world and the freshly-unburdened intelligentsia had to live without the mediation of gods and divine essences? Hypocratic medicine at the time of Galen was probably more advanced than it was nine hundred years later, even under the famous Moslem doctor, Avicenna. In 200 BC, the other sciences were not unduly inhibited, but their moment of occlusion was soon to come. So what would have happened if the hocus-pocus solutions to important questions were eliminated? Certainly there would have been no refuge for fashionable intellectuals in the mystery cults or subsequently in Christianity – no 'cop out' from a day's pragmatism into a night's fantasy. Human intelligence, inventiveness, and energy would not have been sacrificed along with the Church's smoking incense to make man's fantasies seem true; they would have had to remain earthbound working on man's 'earthly' existence: sanitation in place of exaltation, clothes instead of vestments, doctors instead of saints – the list is lengthy!

The Faith Answer is a carefree haven for tired intelligence. Within its discipline, people can appear to be original thinkers when, in reality, they are merely rearranging the founder's prejudices. Society itself would be greatly frustrated by the closing of these havens. Once established and co-opted by society, they represent extremely handy systems for control. Christianity, generally regarded by the Roman State as an enemy because it challenged the establishment, went from being persecuted in AD 275, to tolerated in AD 313, to becoming itself a persecutor in AD 325. When one system sufficiently demonstrates its strength, which is essentially its ability to force homogeneity of belief on people, society will accept it. A society denied the use of such a system would be prevented from exercising its usual technique of domination. It would be forced to develop forms of cohesion based on its usefulness to individuals.

Augustine[8] wrote his *City of God* partly as a consolation prize for the survivors of the AD 410 invasion of Rome. He said (roughly paraphrased): 'Forget the values of the City of Man – the important city's up there...' Of course, this sort of thinking was a boon to invaders. In AD 476, people barely noticed the removal of the last Western emperor, Romulus Augustulus. Meanwhile, over in the East, in New Rome – Constantinople – there reigned a combination of Church and State, an embrined society, occasionally, although painfully, shaken from its lethargy by disputes between Holy-Image lovers and Holy-Image haters (the inconoclasts), assorted heresies, and military assaults.

It is scarcely necessary to add that scientific theorizing and technological applications ceased. These centuries were wasted opportunity. In the West, some fairly interesting squat statues and illuminated manuscripts were produced; in the East, manuscripts, icons, and mosaics – not much return for all those years. Contrast the accomplishments of the two-hundred year period of 'disillusionment' after the Peloponnesian War with the twelve-hundred-years of established, uncontested Christian certainty, AD 325 to Copernicus.[9]

The Faith Answer is, to borrow a psychoanalytic term, the epitome of the *'causa sui'* project. It believes itself to be an immortal absolute a completely Promethian totality to which all things are required to relate. Why should such a deity do more for man than accept his praise?

8 Chart point 11.
9 Chart point 40.

78

2. Fashion

Anyone who has been a member of a university faculty will be aware of the pervasiveness of prevailing intellectual fashions. These fashions come and go almost as easily as clothing fashions and are sometimes associated. And yet it doesn't seem that man has made this simple connection. After all, who would kill someone whose trousers were old fashioned?

It is customary to be tolerant of clothing fashion, at least in places where an intellectual or Faith Fashion does not dominate. If religious intellectual ideas are recognized as nothing more than fashions subject to change and replacement, how can extreme measures of conformity be justified? It is just as though a clothing fashion-house announced that its new spring line was going to be permanent, that everyone would wear it forever, and that all other fashion houses would be closed down. How the customers would laugh! But, of course, if the mannequins next stepped off the stage wielding automatic weapons, we would see the critics and cynics getting into the new line, perhaps even with a word of praise here and there.

Toward the end of Louis XV's reign, French court ladies, following the style of Marie Antoinette, kept raising the height of their coiffure until special carriage doors had to be built. In the 16th- century, Florentine noblemen wore fur throughout the hot summers. In 1908, American Panama Canal executives could be seen working in hot three-piece suits and stiff collars despite the tropical heat and disease. In the early 1950s ladies' steel-tipped spike heels seriously damaged building floors and the style continued, even though doctors warned of spinal damage from the heel to occiput shock transmittal. In the l9th-century cinch corsettes became so popular and so tight that the 'ladies' frequently fainted. The deaths of Chopin and other fashionable artists from 'consumption' even made it fashionable to look tubercular. As late as the 1920s, Thomas Mann's *Magic Mountain* still invokes the ambience of modish death.

These fashions are obviously absurd, but only as to degree.

When an important Fashion House introduces its new line,

it usually writes up a rationale for it. This is a fascinating document, seething with white-hot enthusiasm and confidence in the lasting quality of the innovation. The whole House is primed and excited. Even the languid models have been hyped up for the occasion. Just as everyone was for the last one. The buyers are supposed to catch this excitement and flood the shops with this 'new look'. The more permanent the potential change appears to be, the bigger the order. At a certain point, if the new mode is being widely bought and appears to be 'going critical', the most unfriendly buyer will have to order it. So it proceeds outward, insidiously, from the core of zealots to the most reluctant. At the beginning of a radically new fashion, many people laugh at the wearers:

'She looks ridiculous in those clogs!'

'It's just an attention-getting device.'

'I hope she breaks her ankle!'

Then a little later, as the shops flood with all kinds of clogs...

'You know, basically I don't like them, but this yellow pair isn't too bad.'

A month later, the critic, along with thousands of others can be seen hobbling down the Champs-Elysees in bright yellow clogs, and she has even persuaded her 'hopelessly conservative' mother to buy a pair.

Man is a social animal; his values derive from his interaction with other human beings. Fashion is an easily observable demonstration of this fact. Because fashion is accepted and rejected with sufficient rapidity, it is possible to see its coming and goings on a small time-scale. The building institutionalizing and replacement of major Faith Answers usually require many years, which makes the process from man's short time span harder to observe. But the establishing mechanisms of both Faith and fashion seem to be similar.

Since there have been fashions that ran from nudity to total body covering, from hats to cranial deformation, from bare feet, bound feet, to stilts, it should not be surprising to find that Faith fashions have gone from believing in trees to economics, from embalming to suttee, from adoring snake statues to smashing mosaic portraits. It is all there – just a question of telescoping the time intervals to see the absurdity, and then maintaining the same perspective to see the new nonsense when it appears.

The latest fashion in ideas draws forward those persons, who will give 'sworn evidence' its favour. If it is fashionable to see weeping virgins, flying saucers, ubiquitous sexual harassment in the work-place, communist conspiracies – 'Reds under beds', miraculous Faith-cures, witches on broomsticks, covens dedicated to 'ritual' child abuse, etc, witnesses in their droves will come forward. They will resemble one's neighbours; they will often be very convincing, because they, themselves, will, usually, be convinced.

How does this happen? How are, apparently, normal intelligent people taken over by, what, in time, can be seen to be demonstrably ridiculous?

Getting to the absolute bottom of this 'transaction' is probably impossible, but there are certain given elements that are always present. First the delusion must have at least a grain of social acceptability. Second: there has to be some potential pay-off for bearing witness – such as gaining social kudos, impressing friends, material gain etc. Third: the 'witness' must have a subliminal pre-disposition to perform this 'reconstruction' of reality which makes their eye-witness' testimony possible.

The disposition to alter reality exists in practically all human beings. The taking of alcohol, recreational drugs, hyperventilating to enter semi-trance states, the acceptance on trust of stories that seem to run counter to the possible, all reveal a widely proliferated tendency to escape this world's unromantic and iconoclastic 'facts of life'. All that is needed is a set of conditions which provide a potential adept with an excuse to overcome the inhibitions of 'claustrophobic' reality and leap into the latest social dream-fashion. In the the 'flying saucer', example mentioned earlier, the general appearance of such objects had already been sketched out in story and film; so not much imagination was needed to describe them; hence an 'amazingly' homologous co-incidence in the tales told. The grain of truth necessary was that an interplanetary visit was not impossible. The incentive to 'see' might have been a write-up in the local newspaper or even a TV appearance. And so a 'normal' 'everyday' farmer responding to a little summer lightning an invisible jet engine sound, and possibly a beer too many became a witness to a 'sighting'.

Those who stood calling for their leader at the great 1934 Nuremberg rally were by no means all convinced Nazis. Many were there because it was 'the thing to do' because other people were doing it. The Nazi Faith fashion had 'gone critical'. Who could have distinguished amongst the *heiling* thousands the less-committed, less-believing *'sotto voce' heils?* And, such is the composition of crowd hysteria that, bullied and excited by the general frenzy, those less committed fashion followers would soon have been bellowing out with the rest. A few years later, at Second World War body count, the corpses of sincere believers and fashion followers were also indistinguishable. If only Faith 'fashions' did not kill and divert man from his self-development, they could be treated like clothing or hit tunes.

Fashion wraps...   ...and unwraps.

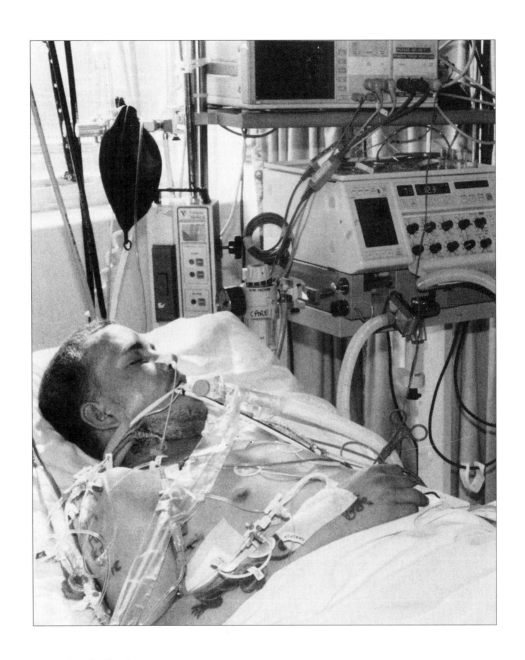

How much alive?

Chapter Six
HUMAN EXISTENCE –
CELLULAR EXISTENCE

Human existence is not the same as cellular existence, although the former requires the latter. A person, depending on the condition and usage of the senses, is either more or less alive. Faith Systems invariably restrict the variegation of existence as well as the permitted usage of the senses, and so actually diminish the existential possibilities of individuals. This reduces the humanness of their existence towards the merely cellular.

Man, in some degree, possesses a duality of his own creation. He is alive because his body is alive. But, as Descartes[1] pointed out, he is also alive because he is aware that he is alive. Who, then, is this 'he' who is aware he is alive? He is not the body, although he depends on the body for his support. He may decide to kill the body, enslave it, mortify it. He behaves like its proprietor. He, the cognitive self, appears to be the 'resident owner' of the body.

If man does have this dual existence, then the human existence of the 'owner', the cognitive self, may be distinguished from the cellular existence of the body.

Success or failure for a biological entity is measured by the extension, continuance or termination of its function or functions. In single-cell units there is little to go wrong, so the measure is, 'Is it living, or has it died?' As the systems increase in quantity of cells and differentiated function, judgement of success or failure of the whole must take into consideration the functioning of the parts, some of which are so essential that their failure, if not remedied, will bring about the failure of the whole.

Functioning heart, lungs, kidney and liver, are all critical to the success of the human unit. There might even be some statistical manner of quantifying degrees of success or failure by

[1] Chart point 47.

assigning numerical weighting to each of its multifunctions.

Death would have to mean absolute failure. But how should the termination of cognition be rated? On the 'analizometer', the heart reads 70%/ breathing oxygen-aided 50%/ kidney with machine 60%/ liver 65%/ digestion not in use due to direct fluid feeding/ocular reflex below 10%/no auditory reaction/no speech or sound except that caused by laboured breathing across the vocal chords/no tactile response except the galvanic through electro-stimulation/EEG reading practically flat. What does this mean in terms of failure or success of that particular human unit? Are not those 'heroic' measures underway out of a disregard for the values of cognition? The doctors are fighting to save a body not a mind. If this person's brain response is irreversible, what are those doctors doing? A horse is often shot for breaking its leg, and a human being with no possibility for restored mentation is 'kept alive'. Behind a privacy screen lies this unit of cells whose basic function is medically assisted. No one can communicate with it in any way, nor can it produce more than minimal autonomic responses to physical stimuli. As a collection of cells, technically it has not yet died, but beyond that, it has ceased to be. Its complete inability to receive or send messages, verbally or non-verbally, robs it of all human characteristics, except its physical presence and the recollections an observer may bring to it.

Surrounded by an interdependent complexity which increases exponentially as the search for keys, answers and simplicity continues, man tries to impose yes or no definitions everywhere he can. This speeds up classification at the expense of both qualitative and even quantitative information. A census-taker passing by the hospital would list the impossibly-damaged aggregation of cells lying in 'Intensive Care' as living, just as much as the doctors and nurses attending to the tubes and dials. But suppose the criteria were changed, and the census-taker, after conferring with the medical support team, put down 1% alive. Then collecting percentages from this and other hospitals, put together out of one hundred such 'patients', a statistic of, say, three 100% people, how ridiculous the statistic would be. With mentation remaining intact, the doctors have a real person to save, not merely an agglomeration of never-knowing cells. Incurable and mentationless unconsciousness is subjective death – the permanent incapacity to know or make known. The mentationless cell-collection possesses the topography of humanness, but it might as well be a carefully arranged flesh-toned mass of amoeba cells. It is not really a person, although it is technically not yet a corpse. Looking at an electro-encephalograph which hour after hour shows flat waves, it might be permissible to put Descartes' famous 'Cogito ergo sum' into the negative third person – 'Non cogitat ergo non est' (He does not think; therefore he is not). This seems reasonably clear. But if the presence of brain activity means that there is humanness in a body, that may be still a minimal criterion if there be no registration of sense input. It is this registration and reaction to the messages of the senses that confers (non-technical) recognizable humanness upon a living body.

A human being is known, apart from a characteristic physiognomy, to others and also to himself, as possessing a distinct reactive frame for dealing with sense input. This is the foundation of what people call their self-image. It is constructed out of the brain's interpretation of a myriad of sense messages since, and probably before, birth. It is resistant to sudden alteration, but not at all impregnable. That its maintenance requires the individual's discretionary use of his senses has been shown by so-called 'brain washing' and results of prolonged solitary confinement.

Experiments in sensory deprivation have shown that without constant sense-reportage of the environment, severe mental dysfunction occurs which, in some cases, can even be permanent. The subjects feel 'unreal', and yet their senses have not ceased to function, the experimenters have only devised ways of minimizing the variation of their messages. If there is sound, it is always the same, the temperature of $37°$ C water in which the subject may be suspended never varies, nor the aroma of the room, etc. The restriction, cutting off, or substitution of sense data is capable of causing profound alterations in the person affected.

Human existence is not in the undamaged cell-structure of the ear drum or retina but in their utilization: it is the effusion and intake of perception. This is the true discriminant of a *person's* existence. It is, therefore, beyond the cells of the basic support system, the human *sine qua non.* To take even part of this from man, or impose restrictions upon it, is to diminish his existence, to reduce him in the direction of a mere cell aggregate.

This argument is an attempt to distinguish between cellular and human existence. The latter depends on the former, but the reverse is not true. The discriminant of human existence is the functioning of the senses – a Faith Answer actually 'nationalizes' the senses to as great a degree as possible, thereby actually reducing the adept's human existence – his senses become part of the cell structure of the Faith Answer.

If all the sense receptors are working equally in two people, for instance, their hearing, sight, etc., and one uses them with enthusiasm and curiosity, while the other lies endlessly dozing on a bed, existence for the utilizer of the senses is qualitatively much expanded over the sleeper's. The point can only be made through broad examples because, otherwise, distinctions become wastefully subtle. Questions like 'Should Napoleon also have taken singing lessons?' or 'Should Einstein also have studied cooking?' lead one to ask whether this would have qualitatively increased their existence? Perhaps, but it is easier to see the function of sense suppression or utilization in larger terms: the thousands of nuns and monks on bread and water, not even allowed to touch themselves, let alone others, staring endlessly at the same holy pictures, wandering around the same cloister, mumbling the same words, living a life deprived of sense perception. What they received in return from their Faith Beliefs may have seemed worth it to them, but even they would agree that they lived as little in the world as possible and, therefore, their sense perceptions of the world were correspondingly reduced. In both a quantitative and qualitative way, their existence in this world was diminished – a part of which was given over to their Faith Belief. This was really their affair. But what about the people who trembled in front of local priests, whose lives were at the disposal of the Church/manor establishments, who didn't even have the privilege of leaving or deciding if they liked it, who were trapped by law, church and education? These people, too, lived a diminished existence due to the demands of a Faith belief which never offered them a choice.

A Faith Answer system maintains its existence through donations, forced or seduced, from its members. What is actually handed over is part of an individual's own existence. His autonomous sense-expansion, in proportion to his dedication, ends; and as much as possible of the sense autonomy he had is given away. Many promises are made to the contributors – heaven on earth or in the sky. Like blissful retirement programmes that never happen, the adept saves and scrimps his time and existence, or is forced to for the sake of the world's oldest con game – Faith Answer promises.

Should Napoleon also have studied singing?

Chapter Seven
ORGANIZATIONS AND THE 'FULL' LIFE

There is a growing frustration felt by many people over their inability to influence the course of both technology and political life. The fear of being 'taken over' is not baseless, Individuals, who have no independent stance for judging, risk being trapped by the imposed objective criteria of Faith Answers. Unless objective criteria that relate to individuals' subjective requirements are constructed, those individuals will remain defenceless in the face of Faith Systems.
1. Objective Criteria in a Subjective World
2. The Defenceless Individual
3. The Subjective Imperative

The survival of the human species on its present population-scale without the organizational structure essential to an advanced technological society today would be impossible. Without such a structure a substantial percentage of the earth's population would be condemned to death.

Those who wish to dismantle the technological society allege humanitarian reasons without following through the effects of their 'policy'. Anarchism or the elimination of organizational power-control is also motivated by humanitarianism. Its 'dis-organizational' effect would be similarly disastrous for the 'have nots' of the world since technology, without its organizational megastructure and infrastructure, would be unable to function.

What is behind these attacks on applied science and social decision-making is the feeling that there is an inability to control the decision-making process and that people feel that technology functions as a self-perpetuating, self-justifying monster capable of destroying 'human' values. Part of the reason is the vastly increased world population. This in itself prevents most individuals from having a perceptible share in decision-making or gives them, as in large centralized democracies, so small a share as to be practically worthless. In addition, the rate of scientific discovery and technological application has increased so markedly that a great majority of people have been left far behind in any comprehension of even the under-pinnings of the technology of their time. As a result, most of the world no longer lives surrounded by the ancient mysteries which so baffled man, but by new, man-made mysteries.

There is a cure for this malaise – find out, learn. But it is extremely unlikely that most people will take this course. The lazy will thus become victims of their laziness and succumb to the mass-manipulation capability inherent in modern high-technology.

The 'old time' Faith in the 'people' so quixotically displayed by the French Revolutionaries of 1789 has yielded more and more to hypocritical lip-service and not-so-private contempt for the masses.

Whether man likes it or not, an elite is emerging which may use the forms of democracy to govern, but not the substance. After all, what executive would consult with ignorant advisors and expect to receive valuable suggestions? The important gap in Western society is not between generations, or at least it is not so caused; it is a knowledge gap where those who have freshly learned the technique of running a high-technology society cannot communicate satisfactorily with those who are ignorant of it whether they be contemporary or belong to other generations .

It is unlikely that the activists fighting science, technology and, to a much less-significant extent, the anarchists attacking group-power, realize that their goals achieved would mean the death of perhaps half the world's population. Both anti-technologists and anarchists are really struggling with impotence. The autochthonous logic of technology combined with the self-perpetuating autarchy in the controlling group, together with the 'ignorance gap', leave individuals hopelessly clutching at their unavailing democratic straws.

Since the 4th-century BC man has developed no basically new political theories, despite the enormous alteration in all other methodologies. A kind of Russian roulette is played again and again with the same political forms that were put forward by Plato and Aristotle, neither of whom made allowance for the political effects of population growth or technological change.

The highly-praised, 5th-century Athenian democracy required 'total immersion' of its citizens to function properly. It was really a political religion. The 1960s hippie ideal was non-political – a dropping out from 'the system'. In the first case, individuals, to have a say in the running of the State, must dedicate themselves totally to it and, in the second, by dropping out, they risk being 'taken over' by the existing political force.

It is easy to say that the answer lies somewhere in between; but as long as Faith Answers exist, both silent majorities and drop-outs are liable for conscription. How would anyone achieve such a 'balance', for example, during the social convolutions set in motion by Mao Tse-Tung in China or the Moslem revivalism of Khomeini and his successors in Iran?

Who knows how long the 'storm' of Faith will continue?

When Constantine gave Christianity its 'green light' in AD 313, how or where did one lie low? Christianity went on and on gathering power through close to thirty life-times. Still, for a great part of that period, except for relatively brief moments of extreme religious exaltation, it would have been possible to live without 'over-doing' the religious side of life – lip service and church attendance; living without believing in Christian mythology. But it could be argued that this policy of disbelief and laying low will do nothing to develop individual potential within the current social context. This is from both an individual and social point of view a serious criticism, since it contains the core of man's subjective-objective dilemma.

1. Objective Criteria in a Subjective World

People adapting to a given situation tend to appraise their current happiness through comparisons between themselves and those they believe to be part of their peer group. In the extensive literature of concentration-camp inmates, no one envied the almost untouchably distanced SS guard. What mattered were ones' companions in horror. Someone obtained extra food, managed to keep a little dignity, had better clothes, better work assignments. These were the measuring sticks. In the early Middle Ages, with no point of comparison beyond their peer group, people settled for a paltry existence inside the continuum provided by the Church-Baron complex.

Unless man can point to his own individually-oriented objective criteria, he is eternally trapped in a kind of confused subjectivity (or the 'objective truths' of a Faith Answer), unconsciously imprisoned without appeal. The paradox here seems to be that if the Existential-Freudian-Einsteinian contribution to thought led 20th-century man away from objective criteria, apparently relating and concentrating all meaning upon each separate individual, it also robbed those individuals of any objective consensus outside that forcibly imposed by the power of a reigning Faith Answer. Instead of serving as a protection to individuals, enabling them to build a world of personal values, the priests of subjectivity have tended to bless an anarchy of values turning people uselessly in upon themselves until they fight to break into some prison of objectivity where all values are set by the governing Faith Answer.

Fortified by all the rationalizing powers of a fine intellect, Sartre, the apparent quintessence of 20th-century subjectivity, tried to be a Communist as well. He, of all people, should have realized that Communism was a typical Faith Answer requiring total submission to discipline. But living outside the immediate reaches of its political power, he could escape the fates of Mayakovsky, Mossolov, Prokoviev, Eisenstein, Gorki, Meyerhold,[1] and others. Like Picasso, Diego Rivera, Orozco, Luchino Visconti, Jean Paul Luc Goddard, Passolini, and other Western artist-intellectuals, Sartre sported the shoulder-boards of Marxism without seriously submitting to its discipline, receiving the salutes of high rank without ever having to join the army.

That Sartre found it necessary to adopt such a self-imposture as being a Marxist and simultaneously an existentialist, is highly symptomatic of the malaise of existentialism. There seems to be no usable ground between the two ideas. One is almost

(cont. from p94)
Vsevolod EmilievichMeyerhold (1874-1942), theatrical producer and astonishing innovator of theatrical experiment, began running into serious trouble in 1932 with a *Pravda* ('truth') denunciation of 'experiment in the arts' as a form of decadence. In January 1938 his theatre was closed. He was set up in June 1939 to say 'mea culpa' at a meeting of the All-Union Convention of Theatre Directors but, instead, defended the right of creative artists to experiment and criticized state policies of uniformity. He was quickly arrested and sent 'north'. Soon afterwards, his wife was murdered, with her face disfigured. It is not known how he died.

without objective criteria and the other, being a Faith Answer, demands the merging of all subjectivity into its objective 'truths'. An existentialist disagreeing with party discipline could easily justify opposition based on existentialism's continuing approval of any self-knowing intended individual action. In Sartre's case, he seems to be fleeing from the formless subjectivity of his own philosophy toward the rigid catechism of Marx's objective reality – toward objective standards.

If the years from 200 BC to the late Renaissance were skipped, what standards could be used to determine whether or not the excised period was or was not a waste of time? Are there any shibboleths outside the 'objective realities' offered by Faith Answers? Islam, Buddhism, Marxism (in its 'glory days') and, especially, Catholic Christianity have provided whole catalogues of answers to such questions. Other Faiths, though less catechized, could still produce a batch of answers. But must those who manage to remain outside the fold of a Faith Answer live completely subjectively, incapable of applying objective criteria to history and their own present? This weakness is a power vacuum into which a Faith Answer can move. It is invited.

Is there such a thing as objective reality, or is it the fabrication of man's despair? If each individual is to be regarded as the ultimate totality of his own existence, then all things must relate to him, to his subjective being. Beyond himself there can be no independent meaning. Only as the individual accords existence to something does that thing exist for him. As long as he lives, it too exists. When his life ends, relative to him, all this furniture of his existence will cease to be. It shouldn't be a surprise to find that all supposedly objective 'truth' systems object to Freud's placement of the patient individual at the centre of his private universe – such enshrined subjectivity is ultimately bound to deny the nonrelative values of 'objective truth': '...if it works for me, it is true for me; if it doesn't, then it is false relative to me and my life...' Because it offers a universal 'objective truth', not a relative one, no Faith Answer can tolerate such a relative and pragmatic approach as the logic of subjectivity suggests. If it cannot transcend individual subjectivity, it cannot expect to stimulate the personal sacrifice upon which its apparent objective existence depends.

At Easter, Virgins and Christs may be dusted off and taken through the streets. But they themselves are incapable of motion. They only move through the believers' lifting power. Even though the bearers' legs may be invisible, the onlookers know they are only hidden by a cloth overhang. The same is true of the supposed objective 'truths' of a Faith Answer. The motive force, the *mise-en-scene'* – its very 'existence' is the product of the taking or gifting of the subjective existence of many individuals. Without this sacrifice of self, the so-called eternal 'objective truth' of this *trompe-l'oeil* theatre vanishes.

Only when these gigantic dreams pass is it usually possible to know them for what they were. Only then the dedicated acts of the martyrs seemed wasted and the upholders' bad backs useless. But still, a rationalizing argument for total immersion in some Faith Answer can be heard:

A: 'Isn't it too bad about Joe Faithful?'
B: 'Not at all. He died a martyr's death, believing deeply in the cause.'
A: 'But you and I know Moralities United was nothing but a big business.'
B: 'Yes, true, but he didn't. It all came out after he gave his life.'
A: 'So we deny the absurdity of his sacrifice because he didn't know it was absurd?'
B: 'Basically yes. After all, to him it was beautiful to go that way.'
A: 'So we join in praising what we know is folly!'
B: 'Because to him it was beautiful! It was his life!'

The burden of this discussion shows that without a generally shared technique of self-protection, individuals can be induced to sacrifice themselves to maintain the existence of groups and whole societies. All that is necessary is that the group's objective values become a vital part of the adept's persona, that the adept's subjective needs become equated with the group's requirements, ie. 'God, King and Country!'

Part of the argument over Joe Faithful's sacrifice is that even though Moralities United turned out to be a fraud, he did not know it, and so relative to him and what he knew, the sacrifice was subjectively valid. Most observers, however, would agree that this was more a matter of tragic error than beautiful sacrifice.

The 'tragic error' of Faith adepts, since man's historical record began, has been the ease with which they have been persuaded to surrender themselves to the 'objective truths' of some Faith Answer at the expense of their time, their lives, and, of course, other people's lives.

It is up to the Faith Answer or, for that matter, any power structure, to create such an ambiance in its controlled society that those doing its bidding up and down the ladder of its pecking order will, relative to the rest of the population, seem blessed.

The argument for medieval Christianity, happiness in a concentration camp, and the self-sacrifice of the late Joe Faithful, asserts that relative satisfaction is always present in all societies, and at all times; and the inverse corollary, that there are, outside of a Faith Answer, no objective standards for individual human satisfaction. Put more coarsely, it comes down to: 'What the individuals in a society don't know, won't pain them.' So Stalin sealed off Russia to lock out discordant ideas and experiences.

In this case, man has no way out of the boxes into which he may be thrust by the succession of Faith Answers, and all ways of existing become, relative to themselves and to their particular continuum or context, equally adequate, escaping the criticism of objective criteria.

To what objective criteria can man point? How can he save himself from drowning as an individual in these constant Faith Answer inundations, sanctified by their 'objective truths'?

Man, the individual, must be the judge; his criteria his own existence. Death is failure. It is, from the 'point of view' of the organism, the ultimate catastrophe. Now that life is ended for that particular cell or entity of cells, its former identity is lost in the meaninglessness (from the organism's viewpoint) of death.

That human observers may find meaning in the death of plants and animals and other humans, or even in their own, does not alter the physical catastrophe of death for the organism involved. The death may form a part of the 'grand natural scheme'; it may become food, manure or decoration. If the organism had lived on, it might have disturbed the 'natural balance' of things. None of these over-views can alter the subjective disaster of death. Whatever may be the utility to the rest of the world from the death of an organism – the life that was is no more. That life has come to nothingness.

The fact that all known Earth organisms die does not mean that from their 'point of view' they should. All life fights this oblivion. *En masse* the struggle has been successful; individually, a failure.

An inherent imperative to continue existing seems to be vested in all forms of life. Over millions of years those forms of life better adapted have survived. Within those successful categories of species, individual organisms instinctively fight against their particular oblivion. Without this individual struggle and the genetic inheritance from those organisms relatively better at surviving, their species would not have survived. Man's body is equipped with a variety of control and protection devices 'designed' to maintain life (cellular survival). Like all other living matter, it battles against extinction; producing cells, fighting infection, and carrying on its autonomic functions right up to, and sometimes even after, clinical death.

Man's body does biologically what it can to avoid dying; but what about the 'resident owner' of the body? The cognitive 'self' has also sought to avoid oblivion through noncorporeal ways of surviving. It knows the 'secret' that the body will die and so the self plans its survival by disassociating itself from its moribund support-system. Its inherent imperative for continuance has resulted in a myriad of mass immortality schemes that stretch from the funded banalities of Greco-Roman burial societies, in which, for cash received, the names of the dead were regularly remembered, to the Kamikaze's entry into the Yasukuni Shinto warrior shrine via the funnel of a US warship. These mass-survival projects, which are always Faith Answers, actually diminish the self's present scope of choice.

They are a process by which a group or a whole society, armed with a Faith Answer, works toward its own immortality by selling participation shares to individuals, the price of the shares being present sacrifice for future benefit. The final product is that the Faith-Answer group lives 'through the ages' like Dracula, fed at the cost of its parishioners' human and, quite often, corporeal existence. In order to 'live on' after death, to survive the body's extinction, individuals accept incredible inroads into the 'now' of the human existence.

The attaching of the self to a participation in some form of group immortality whether physical, mystical or political always involves sacrifice. It reduces today's choices for tomorrow's glories. The Nazi saint, Horst Wessel,[2] and the victim of Moralities United will go alike to 'untended' graves, along with ci- devant heroes of the defunct Soviet Union. Hardworking traitors like Kim Philby, 'Sir' Anthony Blunt, Guy Burgess and Donald Maclean who turned over their daily lives to a cause they thought would never die lie victimized by their Marxist illusions.

Man's human existence is characterized by the registration and usage of his sense-perception system. To the extent that he either does not or cannot utilize it, his human existence is reduced toward a mere collection of living cells.

Just as the criteria of a cell's success is extended life, the criteria of human success is maintenance of cognition and extension of sensation of existence. This requires the active utilization of the sense-perception structure. Where the use of the sensing system is restricted by some physio-mental dysfunction, or where the belief police of a Faith has imposed sense-restrictive laws and thought-limitations, those affected individuals suffer a diminution of their opportunity to extend their range of existence. And, depending on the degree of the physio-mental dysfunction or the sense tribute exacted by the Faith Answer, that individual's existence will be diminished toward the merely cellular.

Instead of trying to advance the cognitive self's imperative to exist beyond the death of the body by performing all the

[2] Horst Wessel, 'Christlike socialist' according to Goebbels – although, according to others, he was shot by a Communist over a prostitute's affections – died an official martyr in February 1930, leaving behind the lyrics to the song that was adopted by the Nazi Party – the Horst Wessel Lied.

useless sacrifices and rituals proposed by Faith Systems, individuals could instead channel it into the deepening and amplifying of their actual existence; an existence which is intensive rather than extensive, in which the self is reconnected to the body and the body correspondingly revalued.

The search for the prolongation of existence could then be medical rather than metaphysical. And, while science worked, the self could explore an internal and external world freed from sense-restricting Faith-Answer requirements in concert with the body instead of in opposition to it.

Gathered from the subjective needs of individuals, this standard – the intensive living of the life that is (the 'bird in the hand' life) – can be used as an objective criterion to see how individuals fared throughout history, and which social groupings now or then have come closest to providing such an opportunity for personal expansion. Thus, history may be re-analysed without the automatic obeisance to the great 'movements', the 'warring Titans', and all those colossal monuments; but, this time, we can ask how well individuals came off in those periods.

Let us look for a moment at the life of *Reichsfuehrer* Heinrich Himmler, ruler of the *SS*. It is early 1945, Nazi Germany is losing the war but Himmler's highest ambition has at last been realized – he has been made a Field Commander. His remaining concentration camps are full and disciplined. He enjoys the absolute obedience of the multi-national black uniformed elite lay priesthood of Nazi mythology, the *Schutzstaffeln*.

He has come a long way from the poultry business. (He *was* a chicken farmer.) As *Reichsfuehrer* dreaming dreams, helping to create a new era of splendid 'Aryan' pan-Germanism, was he not fulfiling himself and exploiting his innate potential more than if he were the most successful of chicken farmers? Instead of combining the strains of Plymouth Rock with, say, Rhode Island Red, he could decide questions of human breeding. And, it should never be forgotten, that, if Hitler had won the Second World War, Heinrich Himmler would, almost certainly, have been one of the fixed stars in the Nazi 'New Order' firmament. In this case should we then say *'Reichsfuehrer SS*

Heinrich Himmler, ideaman of Nordic racial mysticism, Liquidator-in-Chief of 6,000,000 Jews, slavemaster of the Eastern *"Untermensch"* really lived his life to the fullest within the given social context of National Socialism?' We must admit that in all probability he would have, unless we insist that life as an agriculturalist would have stretched him even further.

Now on the other hand (to put it mildly), there are those individuals upon whom Himmler's 'full' life was built. In fact, it was, to a great extent, built on their deaths. Those destroyed lives vis-a-vis Himmler's full life easily tip most objective scales against Himmler. But that is because Nazism did not survive. Suppose the 1,000-year Nazi Reich had come to be; Himmler would have been accorded sainthood. Let us fantasize that in the year 2933 it was at last realized, after the 1,000-year Reich was overthrown, that it had been a 'criminal enterprise'; statues of Himmler would be promptly smashed and laser likenesses switched off. But has this late re-evaluation prevented thousands of oppressive killer officials of the system from having lived full lives?

If the social system in power is sufficiently strong it will be the sole pathway to and designator of the 'full life', so that individuals must develop themselves within their society's context or lose this opportunity. And, if the 'Reich' in question lasts as long as 1,000 years, it will be their only opportunity.

What about the possibility of self-realization through opposition? Obviously a very risky alternative with the bonfire, the rack, the 'insane' asylum, the piano-wire noose, the firing squad (if you were lucky) being various exemplary endings to attempts at self-realization through opposition.

Can there be objective criteria without having it originate from some power-hungry social system? Or are we forced grudgingly to admit that Himmler's 'full' life, although lived at the cost of millions, was as valid in its social context as the life of such a human benefactor as Dr. Fleming, who discovered penicillin? Both believed they were doing something of great importance. Himmler believed he was eliminating a genealogical plague – the Jewish bacillus; Fleming fought non-political biological infections. If the Nazi empire had prevailed, both these men would have been honoured (Fleming was British but not Jewish), although one suspects Himmler would have had the 'lion's share of honour'.

Here is the core of the matter. Individuals, by accepting the current 'objective' social criterion for judging good and evil fail to construct their own; so that they are anchorless at moments of social extremism.

Surely there must be some valid objective criteria for judging the life of a Himmler or a Fleming, beyond some contemporary social chorus of praise or blame. Strangely enough this objective criteria is formed from the life-needs of all living individuals. It is a collection of their subjective requirements, the most primordial of which is to continue to be alive. In this sense, the social value of Himmler's 'full' life is immediately impugned and the existence of Fleming praised. That is easy to see, but how is an American bombardier's life to be judged *vis-a-vis* the 80,000 Japanese lives terminated and thousands more terribly damaged in Hiroshima? There is the social rationalization of war. The bomb was dropped to avoid an invasion with its attendant American casualties. At least the lives of 80,000 Japanese may be set against the lives of Americans that would have been lost in the invasion on the beaches of Japan. This is no consolation to the citizens of Hiroshima, but it is to the estimated American losses. The Nazi murder of 6,000,000 Jews had no such 'pragmatic' offset. They were murdered for doctrinal reasons as part of the Nazi Faith Answer.

Second to the requirement of staying alive is the question of how that life is to be lived. Someone locked up speechless in a solitary, soundproof room and fed an unchanging, bare subsistence menu might be kept alive for 200 years without ever experiencing any of the delights of existence. Without a chance to explore and develop themselves, individuals must lead a diminished existence compared with those who have an opportunity to enjoy variegation and take advantage of it. Individuals bereft of the five senses cannot develop any aspect of life experience. As a corollary, societies which offer a minimum of variety are guilty of reducing and minimizing the possibilities of individuals to enlarge upon their potential and widen their existence.

The judging of one society's relative merits vis-a-vis another's should be based on the variety of experience offered to individuals. A society's claims to transcendental efficacy are only advertising gimmicks. They are a deceptive device – a smokescreen behind which heinous crimes against individuals are frequently committed. While the State was withering away, what happened to the individuals trapped in Stalinist and post-Stalinist Russia? While the Nazi 'Super Race' was forming, how did individuals fare? While waiting for the Second Coming and Judgement Day, were individuals given more or less possibilities for sense experience?

If individuals began re-examining societies, past and present, with even these crude yardsticks, social oppression would be impeded. Society might be forced to offer its 'constituents' pragmatic programmes of individual interest instead of transcendental dreams.

Those beautiful, 'Faith-happy' days of the Church/Baronial conspiracy against individuals, the 'edifying' theological struggles of the Byzantine Church, the Trotsky and Maximilist heresies,[3] the tooth-and-nail dispute between the priests of *Ra Horakty* and *Amun Ra*[4] – the list goes on – all consumed individual lives, ending them abruptly or depriving them of their opportunity to live without 'charismatic' interference. A graph of history might be drawn showing the increasing and decreasing societal demands on individuals with the resulting amplification or diminution of their human existence.

For example, looking back at the Napoleonic Wars, which, unfortunately, constituted the Emperor's prime activity, how were the majority of individuals affected? Most of the poor devils spent the time slogging over the map of Europe, turned on from time to time by hand-me-downs from Napoleon's charismatic personality. But the French State loved it. It was a time of enthusiastic obedience. For many French school children, Napoleon is a French 'Alexander the Great'.

And, in the 20th-century charismatic Lenin, that erstwhile patriarch of Soviet Marxism, what did he do for individuals? He presented them with one of the most anti-individual sys-

[3] Trotsky believed (heretically, according to Stalin) that socialism could be built in individual states without necessarily coming under the Soviet Union's hegemony. The Mensheviks (minority party) thought that revolution could be made using the middle-class parties, whereas the Bolsheviks (majority party) refused any such collaboration. In this policy the Mensheviks were much closer to orthodox Marxism.

[4] See Chapter 5, Footnote 5.

tems ever known. 'Power to the people', but not to the individual. And, if none to the individual, then the slogan simply means 'all power to the State'.

2. **The Defenceless Individual**

Unfortunately for human history, most schemes for man's betterment are not restricted to suggestive ethics; they are all too frequently sanctified as objective truths. Generally, in the past, the only escape from the objective truth of one Faith Answer was into the objective truth of its rival. In between was a dangerous, lonely, no-man's land. In the Soviet Communist *auto-da-fe*, the few 'successful' resisters were believing orthodox Christians, the weakest 'sisters' were the hardened old revolutionaries who ideologically had no place to escape. The more they, like Bukharin[5], believed in Leninist-Marxism, the more they found themselves undermined by their Faith Answer's objective truths.

In the Stalinist Purge Trials, Bukharin's absolute absorption in this faith at the expense of his subjective existence meant that he really did not exist outside of it – to be expelled from the Party equalled 'subjective' death – so he ended in co-operating in his own extinction since it seemed the best way he could help.

If the objective truths of a Faith Belief are really nothing but an 'Alice in Wonderland' pack of borrowed cards, having no existence except that collected from the subjective existence of individuals, why can't this fact simply be realised and the revolving door of their comings and goings be dismantled?

Social instinct, death, fashion, intellectual laziness, and the defencelessness of most individuals are the essential five pillars of Faith Answer success. A society uses the Faith Answer not only to herd and control individuals, but also to exploit its own possibility for immortality. The death of individuals tends to give a society continuing power over its mortal members and often slows the perception that a Faith has been invalidated by change. Fashion acts to make the reluctant-to-join feel alienated, and once the Faith Answer has begun to 'go critical',

[5] Nicolai Ivanovich Bukharin (1888-1938), of whom Stalin said in 1923, 'You and I are the Himalayas, the rest are unimportant', was executed after a show trial on 14 March 1938.

it becomes capable of overcoming and even enshrining the most ridiculous of its claims and doctrines.

Just as many people try to avoid manual labour, they also try to escape the 'agonies' of original thinking, much preferring to re-arrange the predigested prejudices of their time and let that pass for insight instead of laziness.

The weakness of individuals comes from their own failure to protect themselves with criteria sufficient to withstand the assaults of 'objective' Faith Truths. They are often laid low by the mechanisms of societal approbation which exhorts and extorts sacrifice in exchange for peer applause. Like the Kamikaze pilots, suicide submariners, and Hizbollah suicide car bombers, individuals lacking defensive criteria can literally be applauded to death.

As a social animal, man derives most of his self-esteem from the approval of others; it is essential to maintain perspective on the sacrifices required versus the personal value of the applause offered. It is hard to believe that there would be any high-wire acts, goldfish-swallowers, guitar smashers, self-immolators or bull-fighters without audiences.

Most individuals live this way except, of course, on a diminished scale, both as to reward and sacrifice. It is possible within a reinforcing social context to persuade a normal person to do almost anything. Those highly-praised ancient Greeks legally practiced infanticide and, in early Rome, the large-scale rape of the Sabine women was officially approved. Aztecs and other Mexican peoples sanctified the eating of human flesh. Shintoist Japanese made suicide into a holy ceremony. Part of Hitler's Faith was Jewish death. Like the Lord High Executioner's list in *The Mikado*, 'the final filling of the blanks, I'd gladly leave to you': infanticide, suicide, genocide, rape, ritual murder, and anthropophagia do make a reasonably impressive start on a list of societal sins against individuals, and the 'normal' man's participation in them is manifest.

The constant aggression of society against individuals is a war acquiesced in mostly by these same individuals. Their ability to resist is impeded by the failure to distinguish between their subjectiveness versus the so-called objective truths of a Faith Answer.

In Oscar Wilde's *The Picture of Dorian Gray*, the utterly amoral Lord Henry drips elegantly decadent and anti-social venom. Dorian listens and absorbs. Then tries it. He remains handsome, and apparently immune to time, only his portrait reflects his 'life style'. People wonder how Dorian appears so untouched when such evil rumours circulate about him! Wilde, both in *Dorian Gray* and in his own life, demonstrates the subliminal penetration of prevailing social propaganda. Dorian Gray consciously lived the philosophy of Lord Henry and, if he had been able, *au fond*, to ignore the values of his time, he would never have let the ghastly changes in the picture upset him. Wilde's own witticisms at his trial for homosexuality wore off rapidly in court and disappeared in prison. The experience destroyed him. His subconscious acceptance of the very societal values he consciously rejected made it impossible for him to see events and attitudes clearly enough to transcend them. Otherwise he would have seen his own guilty reflection in the picture of Dorian and his own tragic genuflection to society. If such a 'decadent' and militant amoralist as Wilde so completely succumbed to social disapprobation, then apparently there is great difficulty in escaping prepared societal positions and thinking outside them.

3. The Subjective Imperative

Societies have throughout time offered individuals a deal: 'Die for us and we'll make your memory immortal. How much better to sacrifice a few years, which is the most you've got, and take the deal, than die unsung in a corner.' But if people start worrying more about the continuation of their existence than that of the group which includes them, no one's likely to take the shoddy deal. God threw Adam and Eve out of Eden before they could become immortal. Homer, in *The Iliad*, his magnificent *Who Was Who* book of martial manners, had Achilles choose the short glorious life – take the deal instead of living for ages. The exemplary primers are legion; they try to make the reader feel like a hog for living on past the age of heroic sacrifice.

Subjectively, however, the transcendental hopes accompanying the rigorous regimens of sacrifice may compensate for the Faith-Answer demands. Joe Faithful being dead cannot know that Moralities Unlted was a fraud. The Nazi saint, Horst Wessel, cannot know that his death was once the excuse for grandiose parades and solemn ceremonies now abandoned and overturned.

The Faith Answer provides a drugged life, an artificial high. It acts like methedrine for activists like the Palestinian suicide bombers, Hammas, or meprobamates for the quietists like the Cistercians. It is no coincidence that contemporary adepts for whatever Faith System find mood-changing drugs suddenly *de trop* – unnecessary. Equally, Faith Answers generally discourage members from drug use, giving all sorts of sensible reasons. But the real explanation is that the Faith Answer is itself a drug, a very powerful hypnotic, and so it regards other mood-changing devices as unnecessary or competitive.

The individual human imperative is to avoid narcosis, the societal imperative to administer it. It is something like *The Invasion of the Body Snatchers*[6] where, if you went to sleep, 'they' would have your soul, turn you into a plant that looked and talked like you, but whose mind was controlled by 'them'. Societal drugging of individuals is packed with promises and opportunities for self-sacrifice. It is particularly important that individuals be persuaded that 'self-fulfilment' is in the direction of the Faith-Answer magnet, so that their sense donations will be willing and substantial. Because of the relatively 'tiny' human lifespan, the 'faithful' have usually lived and died within the Faith without seeing its flaws or the eventual collapse of its 'truths'. Now because of the vast acceleration of the rate of change from the late 18th-century to the latter part of the 20th-century, it is possible to see some of this usually slow process happening in a single lifetime. The militant atheist of the French Revolution could easily have lived on into France's great Catholic revival. A person born in 1820, taught to believe in the Biblical creation story and Christianity, was quite soon challenged by both evolution and dialectical materialism. The spectacular establishing and subsequent collapse of

[6] *The Invasion of the Body Snatchers* (1956) Walter Wanger. Sol Siegel directed the picture, based on Jack Finney's novel.

Communism within eight decades should be a further warning to future 'Faith Heroes'!

This speeding up in the rate of change offers human beings a perspective they have never before enjoyed. Now people can easily observe the absurdity of rival systems of perfection, as well as evaluate the risk to the human and corporeal existence of those who join the "Faithful".

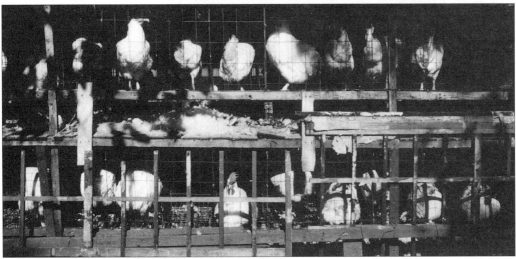

Himmler's
Full Life.
Should he
have stuck
to chicken
farming?

Individual death keeps society strong.

(Frederick March, in 'Death Takes a Holiday', 1934.)

Chapter Eight
DEATH AND THE FAITH ANSWER

Groups can aspire to immortality. Individuals expect to die. By offering individuals a participation in their 'cosmic' survival schemes, Faith Answers can exact absolute obedience. If there were no death, groups would have to offer potential recruits more practical incentives. Faith Answers need individual death to survive.

1. The Group View of Death
2. The Faith Answer and Individual Immortality
3. Society Without Death

1. **The Group View of Death**

A basic list of human requirements always includes food and shelter. Then with these as given, it proceeds to companionship, music, the arts, fanning out to all kinds of more focused preferences. Somebody's bound to add: 'But don't forget, without health, you have nothing'. In *Camino Real*, Tennessee Williams has the owner of the Siete Mares Hotel ask: 'Is life somewhere between light-hearted cohabitation and kids' giggles... are all our memories to go up in smoke... is this what the wheeling heavens turn for?'[1] Dylan Thomas advised: 'Do not go gentle into that good night... rage rage against the dying of the light.'[2] Omar Khayyam, the magnificent drunken fatalist (or as some prefer, the super-Sufi) says, 'Think in this batter'd Caravanserai / Whose Portals are alternate Night and Day, / How Sultan after Sultan with his Pomp / Abode his destined Hour, and went his way.'[3] Shakespeare offers the 'stages of man' speech in which the end comes 'sans teeth, sans eyes, sans taste, sans everything.'[4] Every poet handles death, and man shivers, reading of the mystery, the anger, the fatalism, the cynicism. 'You next,' they say, and they may scream, complain, wonder, or try to explain it, but death, the most wasteful human phenomenon, is the given proposition.

[1] *Camino Real* is a play by Tennessee Williams (1953).

[2] 'Do Not Go Gentle Into That Good Night', Dylan Thomas, *Deaths and Entrances* (1946).

[3] The quotation is from the Edward Fitzgerald 'rendering' (4th edition) of Omar Khayyam's *Ruba' iyat*, Poem XVII.

[4] *As You Like It*, Act II, Sc vii.

The same person who says 'Without health you have nothing' still accepts death as a standard. Man researches all around the edges – curing diseases, fixing up a heart, inventing machines to take over various body functions, 'designing' genes – these same researchers usually accept death as a principle instead of an ultimately curable condition. Intelligent people constantly rationalize death as a good thing, something beautiful, adventurous, peaceful; they usually see it through the left-over lenses of old Faith Belief.

In the 20th-century stories burgeoned and many films were made with themes on those 'anti-social' people who tried to 'cheat' death. In *Death Takes a Holiday*, the moral seems to be that death is really a good thing.[5] Mad scientists, in horror films like *The Man Who Could Cheat Death* and *The Man They Couldn't Hang*, warn the viewer that fooling around with something so 'sacred' as death turns even a decent man evil. The Dracula message seems to be that to 'live through the centuries' like the undead count is not very nice. Worst of all, no classic vampires ever seem to have fun. They go joylessly about their business of regretfully staying immortal. More recently, however, there may be signs that individuals arc becoming less afraid of eternal life than eternal death. The humanizing of the once so fearful figure of Dracula in motion pictures such as *Love at First Bight* is suggestive of this.

Society warns man not to touch the Tree of Life – the fruit is poisonous – see how miserable everyone is who tries it'. 'Foolish Faust' sold his soul to the devil to have his youth back, but naturally everything goes wrong – Gounod's opera has Margareta absolved only in death and Busoni has Faust dying to die.

2. The Faith Answer and Individual Immortality

There is a societal basis for these anti-immortality attitudes. It is doubtful whether a society without death would be able to produce such total allegiance as an immortal society of dying individuals. The critical divergence of objective between the individual and society would be ended – both would be poten-

[5] *Death Takes a Holiday*, American motion picture (1934), Paramount Studios. Directed by Mitchell Leisen. *The Man Who Could Cheat Death*, motion picture from Great Britain (1959), Paramount/ Hammer production, directed by Terence Fisher. *The Man They Couldn't Hang*, American motion picture (1939), Columbia Studios production, directed by Nick Grinde.

tially without death, except that society might find it more difficult to exact obedience to its Faith fashions. The supreme gift that Faith societies have always promised has been immortality for its 'star performers'. What could it now promise adepts to persuade them to make the 'ultimate' sacrifice? A life in the 'hereafter' would look pretty hollow if no one else was expected to join them! Nor would the most spectacular glass tomb, or 'gold-plated' guarantee to live on 'in the hearts of their grateful countrymen' seem like much of a reward to 'new wave heroes' in a society were death was optional.

If the thesis of opposition of goals is accepted between the dying individual and the would-be immortal group, and if it is clear that a society of deathless individuals could not provide much of a reward to the obedient sacrificers, then it is easier to understand why mankind's resources have not been directed toward individual immortality.

Alchemists spent a lot of time trying to turn base metal into gold but, it seems, none at all trying to evoke eternal life. Looking for the philosophers' stone was risky but eternal life would have certainly involved the Inquisition.

In the Biblical story of Adam and Eve, God expelled them from the Garden of Eden not, as most people have been taught to believe, because they ate from the Tree of Knowledge, but because having knowledge, they might 'take also of the Tree of Life and eat, and live forever.'

Would that have bothered God? Perhaps it wouldn't, except that there were human beings writing these words and they, thinking in their human-social way, could see that Adam and Eve would escape control if they became immortal. Why would you need to worship and believe in a god if you already were one?

Society's business, its essence, has always been control, but disguised through great themes of Faith. These themes have been sold as permanent and true for fifty recorded centuries, and yet each one has eventually faded or collapsed, only to be replaced by another. The ally of society has been death. If people had remained alive those five thousand years, it is hard to see how they could be taken in again and again.

Many societies, especially the Christian, have made death seem quite attractive. You couldn't get to heaven if you didn't die, and societies usually make a fuss of the individuals who die for them. In October of 1994, a spokesman for the terrorist group Hammas said: "Hammas loves death more than Izaak Rabin and his followers love life." Like their 12th Century forebears, the Assassins, the young sacrificers 'know' that a wonderful after-life is in store for them!

The Charge of the Light Brigade was evidently anachronistic lunacy, but not for the heroes who were wasted: 'Honour the charge they made! Honour the Light Brigade!'

Because man has never been able to do anything about individual death, he has invented stories for himself which society has used for control and manipulation. The Christian religion not only gave a meaning to life on earth, but promised that death would be a gateway to eternal life. As an ultimate coup, it produced Christ as a living example of the conquest of death. The Tree of Life is, technologically speaking, within our time's garden. Because of the conflict of aims between potentially immortal societies and dying individuals, it is unlikely that any such society would agree to undertake this work unless it were robbed of its cohesive Faith Idea without replacement. Then such a project could, like the American 'Man on the Moon' programme, be substituted.

An end to death would eliminate most man-made fantasies as to the meaning of life and the absurd social convolutions accompanying them. Most important, the aims of society and the individual would no longer be directly opposed.

3. Society Without Death

Suppose that human science were able to continue its present exponential rate of discovery and technological application and, as a result, individual death were eliminated; what kind of 'Great Answer' could regiment a society that lived without death? Something apocalyptical, like the expectation of an invasion from outer space? The risk of man losing power to the machines he invented? But these kinds of mass social energizers are of a totally different quality than a Great Answer – they belong more to the category of 'Great Fears' which have always been good for temporary welding. Any Faith-idea based on an 'after-life' would have a sharply diminished appeal if no one died.

In a deathless society it is also probable that tolerance for ideas and systems would be much greater because there would be all the time in the world to experiment. Each system could have its turn – hundreds of years to prove itself.

There is no reason for death except the deterioration of the cell-producing systems which replenish dying cells at a declining rate. Perfectly good cells are produced even in the senile, but not enough, and not enough of the right ones. But soon it will be possible to clone ultimately complex living organisms, so that precisely the same physical structures may be endlessly replicated, or even altered, losing the experience, and learning of the donor cell system. Where that potential for 'creation' and modification leaves the 'Creator' is a 'theological' conundrum comparable to the past impact of 'heliocentricity' and 'evolution' on the established Judeo-Christian related religions. If cloning cannot be regarded as immortality it is structurally close to it.

Even if immortality were a thousand or more years away, it could still be used as a shibboleth for the absurdity of all Faith Answers. If at this time the sacrifices for dead Faiths don't seem clearly in vain, move ahead into a hypothetical moment when some scientist announces the elimination of death. Where would the Martyrs of the Cross be? – or the Aztec warriors, Mayan girls drowned in holy wells – the Kamikazes of all Faiths! And, on a lesser scale of sacrifice, consider all those hours wasted praying, listening to the priests of all Faiths diffusing their propaganda. A risky investment of precious time which can be invalidated by a single technological development! It seems unwise to accept sensory deprivation for a Faith Answer that must die and one day even be thought ridiculous.

A society which has the possibility of perpetuating itself cannot be expected to urge individual immortality. It will not want to change the power *status quo*. It will continue to push its Faith

Answer as long as individuals can be conned into self-sacrifice. Imagine an Italian scientist, looking up from his laboratory bench, saying, 'I've got it.' The assistants turn excitedly; he announces: 'Eternal life, immortality, the regenerative system, human beings need never die!' The assistants carry the great man on their shoulders to St. Peter's, where a *Te Deum* is hastily improvised. The Pope rapturously refers to this development as a 'miracle to end all miracles'. Then suddenly catching on to the consequences, he orders his trusty Swiss Halbardiers to run the great man and his assistants through. The public gasps and religion is saved.

When death is eliminated, human beings will have to scrap most of their previous philosophico-religious ideas, since the ethical and social goals of all previous societies have to a greater or lesser extent been keyed to the fact of death.

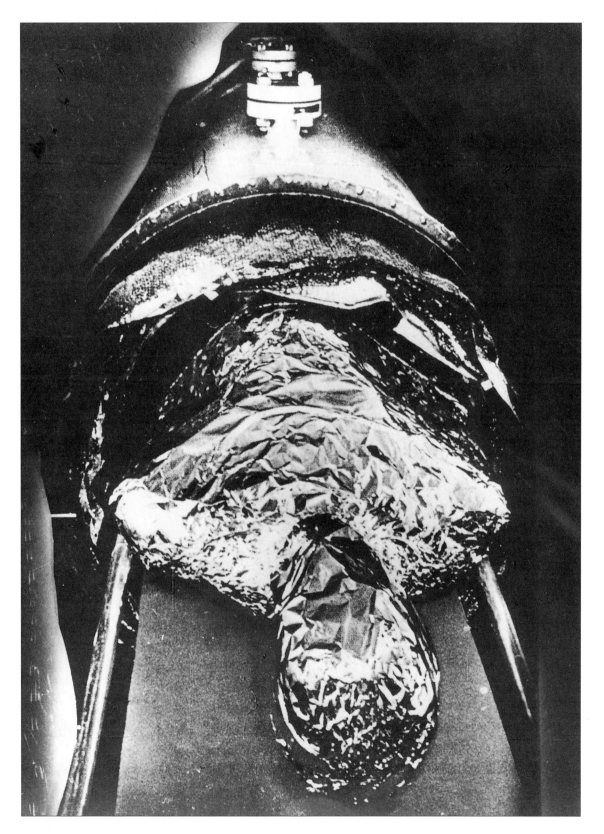

Cryogenics. Frozen hope.

Post-Christian vision. Virgin visions – a declining fantasy.

Chapter Nine
WITHOUT FAITH

Man can manage, and, at times, has managed very well, without a
ruling Faith Answer. Denied its justifying rationale, many despotic
acts are robbed of their raison d'etre.
1. The Stripped Man
2. History Without the Faith Answer
3. Exit Faith, Enter Pragmatism

In presenting a critique of the Great Faith-Answer beliefs, in
attacking them as examples of mass paranoia and enemies of
human development in all its forms, there is the reaction – a
frequently repeated one – that 'man cannot live by bread
alone', that Faith is, in fact, what keeps him together. Remove
this glue, and you end social and individual motivation. It is an
old argument:

'Man would have nothing to fall back on.'
'Except himself and those senses which your new march to
perfection is preparing to enslave.'
'But he would have done nothing significant in all these
thousands of years...'
'Nothing for tourism – no temples, no churches, no pyramids – how do you know he'd have done nothing? He never
had a chance.'
'Without the galvanizing force of Faith, man would be
immobilized. How can you attack something as fundamental
as Faith? You might as well tell us to do without a heart!'

If the heart in the human body doesn't work properly, science tries to obviate it. And if Faith were as fundamental to
man as his heart, then its failure to function beneficially should
be a reason for major questioning. Perhaps instead of being as
important as the heart, it may be more like the adenoids, ton-
sils, or the appendix; something which contributes very little at

this evolutionary stage and can be excised without excessive pain or risk.

It might, like the archaic tail, have dropped off, if it were not for the paranoia-social factor. The potential immortality of a group is connected with its ability to control the membership and the means is the Faith Answer. The universally existing quotient of paranoia, the desire to act without having to question, the anxiety to follow clothing and intellectual fashion as a repository of sociality, identity and security, are all strong reasons for the persistence of participation in Faith Answers.

If these vital but seldom-mentioned elements are disregarded and the historical evidence alone examined, only insanity would explain what various societies have done in the name of Faiths subsequently rejected. The evidence is laid out for anyone to examine. But all societies have tended to suppress basic criticism except at moments of change, when they are weak. Usually the critics belong to the new advancing Faith Answer, or are used by it to help kick in the 'Old Regime' – the rotten infrastructure, the decadent system, the corrupt elite.

There is at this stage much to criticize. It glares out even at a neutral observer. But where were these sages when the movement was fresh, when it was in the full flush of its destructive power? If they had lived in those 'halcyon days', it is quite likely they would have been either silenced by belief or force. Since power writes and rewrites history, critics disappear or are resurrected as heroes at the convenience of reigning Faiths. Unfortunately, most critics arrive like carrion birds over the barely-living body of an old Faith Answer, and are welcomed as though they were catching a fleet enemy instead of just being part of the clean-up detail following some giant parade. Except at these moments, censuring Faith Answers is poorly paid and risky. To attack the principle of Faith itself is a dangerous act of self-isolation. The stones can come from so many directions – so many well-rationalized projectiles. Even people who themselves would be unwilling adepts have been taught by society to believe in belief and admire believers.

In history there are few cases of thunder-lightning deconversions. It always goes 'BAM – I believe', seldom 'BAM –

I don't believe'; unless, of course, it's 'BAM – I don't believe in X because – BAM – I now believe in Y.' There is seldom any organized debaptizing, deconfirming group which does not sell some other Faith. Therefore the ex-Faith-trippers will find themselves arriving without a welcoming committee; no speeches, no band, no laid-on transportation or entertainment. There will be no group interested in them – they will be pariahs insulted as cynics, not even dignified as anarchists. But they will have penetrated to a place where the paradoxes of existence are no longer hidden by the legerdemain of Faith. They will be closer to the truth. The balance between their choices will be at least undisturbed by semi-conscious references to some Faith Answer. The invitation is to abandon, to avoid, to go home, to separate, and then, alone without illusion or crutches, to begin to put together through untainted senses, a fresh reality composed of needs that are personal and not imposed from some Faith grid.

Absolute criteria for action is a Faith Answer fantasy. Who can say whether such and such a course is right or wrong? What may have seemed to be true and right at one time, seems wrong and absurd at another; perhaps later it will be seen as good. A single act might reverberate for hundreds of years, changing and affecting generations, sometimes judged by them as beneficial, at other times pernicious. In the longest view, only the last intelligent member of the human species might be able to say that this or that act, perhaps 100,000 years before his lifetime, had been good or bad, valid or invalid; only he might see which skein of conduct may have led to extermination. Still, he would be forced to judge as a member of the human species. He would not be able to know whether or not, cosmically speaking, the disappearance of man was right or wrong. Impatient man with his black-white, yes-no thinking preferences tends to avoid this kind of disturbing speculation, preferring the convenience of a Faith Answer. There the criterion is always clearly present or ready to be looked up in the catechism. Here no act needs fundamental weighing; no act is tempered by doubt.

The earth's reflected light energy, unlike sound, can never be completely lost. It travels on, away from earth, to be perceived perhaps in the future by nonterrestrial intelligences.

If the observers' equipment permitted sufficiently fine tuning, they could, depending on their distance in light years away from the earth, watch all human history; but without sound, so they could only wonder at the reason for all these activities. They could watch wars, pogroms and all the cruelties of the Great Faith Answers without the rationalizations. No persuasive speeches or argumentation would get through. They would notice that, quite frequently, large numbers of human beings collected together stand still while one person gesticulates and moves his mouth. A little while afterwards people attack one another and die.

If human beings would now remove the rationalizing words, the horrendous acts alone would remain – the ghastly means; never the promised end.

The Faith Answer exists only in words which reverberate away or lie silently in books, rationalizing new actions; the means remain strewn across time, monuments to man's quixotic dreams, inexplicable to an independent observer.

1. **The Stripped Man**

A person who has 'stripped' from his life the conditioned vestiges of Faith Systems past and present appears anti-social, and he almost is. He is only as social as he must be. He is always looking for balance: to give up even a small part of sense autonomy to a group must be a carefully balanced decision between the benefits and dangers. His suspicion of groups, even non-Faith associations, will make him temper his allegiances. But a group with limited goals which takes only what it reasonably needs from its members could be joined. The sense apparatus and its extensions gain importantly from social interplay. To become a hermit is to deny these possibilities, just as surrendering to a Faith Group damages or ends individual sense-development. Neither alternative offers balance or limited participation, therefore both must be rejected.

After the procession of Faith Answers and their ecstatic

visions, the view of the 'stripped man' may seem bleak. Once there were gods in trees, brooks, the sun and moon, and the wonderful tales of the past when man could talk to a god, when a god even looked like a man or at least a familiar animal. In the tomb of Rameses VI, far below the desperate dust and heat of the Valley of the Kings, on barrel-vaulted stone and gesso, is the Egyptian sky-goddess, Nut, surrounded by her stars; below that night-blue sky is Tefnut, the goddess of the day, painted on the king's sarcophagus.[1] In that cool pristine place, believers placed the body – even now their belief seems beautiful. The great grisaille rose window of Chartres, the arching sculpture around the doors, the silence of the old crypt, is the ultimate setting for belief. Yet no one now believes in Nut and Tefnut, and Chartres has far more tourists than pilgrims.

To the old Faiths of the world, the new man of Faith says:

'Your ideas are all fascinating nonsense; but I still love your art, your iconography, some of its really beautiful.'

The old Faiths reply:

'What about your Faith Answer? Is that also fascinating nonsense? '

'What do you mean? How dare you! My Faith Answer's truths are provable absolutes.'

That angry character doesn't believe in Nut and Tefnut or the god of Chartres because he believes in something else. His Faith Answer will one day be considered ridiculous, but only because it has been superseded by another.

Because a belief is decorated with exquisite paintings, sculptures and temples, and offers the most seductive logic and the most perfect of ends, does not mean it is true. Standing under Rameses' stars, by the doors of Chartres, or in a frescoed Etruscan tomb, where death seems to be a festive affair, it is easy to wish it were so, to wish that Nut of the night sky was really there, that the wonderful saints of Chartres would be waiting, that there would be gay Etruscan parties in the Netherworld, and more recently, that Marx would get rid of the State.

The Christian might call the Egyptian religion absurd, a kindly Marxist might say the same for Christianity, but no one

[1] Rameses VI (1150-1145 BC) was a pharaoh of the XXth Dynasty in decline. He wisely usurped the tomb of his predecessor, being on a short string economically, but was generous enough to allow commemorative services for Rameses V to continue in the usurped premises. As an aside, the barrel-vaulting in this tomb prefigures by a thousand years subsequent Western world architectural techniques – prefigures because it cut into existing rock and so needed no key stone, but it shows how old is the aesthetic desire for vaulting.

can see absurdity in their own Faith Answer. Christ said, 'I am the way, the truth, and the light.' A Marxist would certainly have denied this, but when pushed by argument might say that 'Marx is truth'. The most perfect blindness coincides with perfect belief. Marx the philosopher announces that all systems have within them the seeds of their own destruction; then Marx the theologian continues. 'Except mine.' He doesn't exactly say it that way, but he does exempt his system from his own weighty observation. And even today after the collapse of the Soviet Union, with the Chinese Communists telling their 'business men'; 'It's OK to be rich'! committed Marxists will say that 'true' Communism has yet to be tried. Faith dreams die hard.

So if the stripped man does not offer religious paintings, architecture, immortality, or social perfection, should his undecorated view of existence be rejected? Are ideas to be chosen for their beauty and paraded on a ramp like a fashion show? The same model has been showing different clothes with different masks for thousands of years, and each new group of buyers over-orders for eternity, forgetting how the fashions change.

The stripped man's view shows the ancient model nude. It offers no way out of questioning contemporary ideas, motivation and social desiderata. It makes choice uncomfortable. It spoils the easy ruts of conduct and belief. It tells no fairy stories, paints no religious pictures, builds no temples. But then, it has nothing to hide, no need for beautiful legerdemain, or people to control with its promises. No celebration necessary.

When someone is asked, as in the story of *The Emperor's New Clothes*, to see something that his senses clearly tell him is not there, Faith can dress the Emperor. Faith over-rides the observations of the senses to produce all classes of delusion. The kinds of delusion depend on the current belief fashion.

Starting in the 1950s, far more 'flying saucers' began to be observed than 'blessed virgins'.

In 1980, doubters of Sovietized Marxism were treated to what seemed to them an incredibly brazen lie: that the Afghan government had asked for Soviet troops to enter their country.

But this apparent lie was not designed to convince doubters; it was more for the congregation of the faithful whose belief in Soviet Marxism was sufficient to accept the story as gospel. (A quick coup d'etat was arranged to 'ratify' the 'invitation')

The delusions sustained by Faith may be weeping virgins, green spacemen or engraved troop-invitations – the possibilities are endless. But the social problem created by these delusions is the great, almost psychotic need of the 'deluded' to initiate other people into their fantasy world; hence all Faith Systems are or have at some time been messianic.

Generally man's Faith delusions have been much more exciting than facts. Who wouldn't prefer to die 'in the sure and certain hope of resurrection' than just die <u>period</u>. For man to be the reason for the existence of other animals, plants, and his Earth to be the centre around which everything moves, is more attractive than being a product of unplanned evolution and Earth being a very minor planet in a minor solar system in an off-corner of one of many galaxies, obeying the orbital motion laws like everything else.

If, to man, truth be stranger than fiction, it has seldom been as attractive. The behaviour of the *pi meson*[2] in high-energy physics, the existence of particles whose half-life is only measurable in microseconds, may be unusual, even fascinating, but it certainly doesn't glorify man. Each scientific penetration of 'mystery' tends to reveal further a reality which is non-homocentric, although paradoxically enlarging the base from which man may increase the power and dominance of his species.

As the body functions become known, as the structure of the environment becomes quantifiable and manipulable, as religions based on racial, economic and other answers are denied by factual evidence, many would-be adepts have retreated into mystical mind-power to find a shelter from scientific technology. The enormous interest in telekinesis, teleportation, telepathy, reading the future, astral influences, comes at a moment of religious defeat and disillusionment. Whatever truths or half-truths may 'materialize' in this movement, it is to be hoped that man does not succeed in codifying the strands of another unknown into some sort of Faith Answer System. Serious

[2] See Chapter 1, Footnote 13.

doubt must always arise if Faith is required to operate a belief.

It is usually the case that when a person wants some change to take place, subjective requirements are not openly stated; instead there is the invocation of some objective reason for the change. The higher and more sanctified the objective source, the purer and consequently less selfish seem the individual's own motivation. It is the appeal to scripture, not subjective judgement, that is supposed to prevail. None of Stalin's purge trial victims were 'power rivals' or 'personal enemies' – they were wreckers of Marxism – revanchists, revisionists, Trotskyites, etc. The Catholic Church fought Manicheans, Monophysites, Paulicians and Gnostics. As many acts as possible are rationalized 'objectively'. In 1794 Danton, Desmoulins, Herbert and dozens of their followers went to the guillotine not accused of any anti-revolutionary activity, except being a threat to Robespierre.

Remove Christianity, Robespierre's Rousseau, and Marxism as the sanctifying rationale, and what remains? The Inquisition without Christianity, Robespierre without Rousseau, and Stalin without Marx would not have been able to reach over the heads of onlookers for an objective explanation of their acts.

It's easy to lump one's enemies, or simply people who disagree, into the 'fatal' category of heresy, but much harder to trump up ordinary charges against each individual. Once the 'objective truth' of the Faith Answer is denied as a rationale, the would-be oppressor is deprived of his most essential device. The legerdemain is ruined, he is 'in the open'. He has to say, 'I want so-and-so dead.' People ask, 'Why?' He says: 'Because...' They wait... At the end, although he might try trumping up phoney murder or reckless driving charges, he is obviously at the centre of the conspiracy, and few will doubt that he wanted so-and-so killed. In the Watergate cover-up, Nixon lacked a Faith Answer system to hide behind or to front for him. Despite all the practical power of the Presidency, he was exposed.

If the leader is successful in his assassination or pseudo-judicial murder, each person involved in the murder process is denied any serious rationalization of their behaviour. They must face their own corruption and viciousness. Of course, they will cast about for more satisfactory views of their acts, but there will be no handy moral catch-all to help them.

Power must be stripped of superstition, magic and the Faith Answer. In the same way a psychologist attempts to unload his patients' tiresome psychic baggage so that they can see themselves and their lives in reasonable perspective, the absence of appeal to scripture will remove a dangerous obsession from the socio-political structure.

The Renaissance, deriving its impetus from 'pagan Rome', was almost an anti-Christian affair. Russia after the 1917 Revolution seemed about to enjoy a fabulous explosion of painting, writing, music and film when Stalin realized, probably correctly, that the movement, despite its Soviet iconography, lacked sufficient self-censorship, alias 'Socialist Realism'. All Faith Answers in their full power insist that artistic activity be confined to propagandizing the Faith Idea (not the glories of individualism), and the regime that enforces it. They tie everything and every developmental potential to their goals, suppressing all else.

It is true that many people have functioned reasonably well within these restrictive parameters, but then, some people were also able to manage in Hitler's concentration camps. Testing human capacity for sense deprivation should hardly be the result of any societal organization, but the proof of a Faith-Answer's strength is in its capacity to deprive. The obeisance obtained is the insignia of its power. The Aztec warrior voluntarily letting other people rip his heart out, the suicide submariners, the flagellant orders, Kali killers, the carriers of Mao Tse-Tung's 'magic' Red Book, and endless others, have, by their debasement of self, exalted some Faith Answer. When the old Faith dies, these rites of Faith are at last, and too late, seen to be pitiful, absurd, ridiculous, and worse, pointless.

The prognosis for an assault on the Super Truths of Faith Power may not be as hopeless as it might at first seem. They all have the fatal flaw of being tied to some form of stasis. Therefore time is against the defenders. The past has shown that change will eventually outmode them. So that if they do not die, they remain as unimportant, impotent and irrelevant appendages to another age.

Unfortunately man's life-span doesn't permit the assault to be carried on with patient confidence. The thought that 'this too shall pass' may offer some vicarious comfort, but it is more than balanced by the necessity of living on in the narrowness of a Faith-Answer world. Or, still worse, to be trapped between rival kinds of claustrophobia, like a middle class Jew in Second World War Poland, caught between Nazism and Communism. When a Faith Answer has lost its basic power and has been reduced to the level of petty nuisances like the remains of the restrictive American Sabbath Day observance (the 'blue laws'), the vacuum is ready to be filled by a new Faith Answer. Therefore, the assault must be on the whole concept of the Faith Answer, not just the one in power.

Attacking the validity of a current system's premise may only help the next one into power. It is necessary to go beyond the premises to oppose the societal use of this kind of paranoic glue to fix itself at the expense of individuals. The sanctification of every societal act through its reference to an established Faith Answer makes oppression easy.

When the details of the magician's tricks are known, how patter and hand gestures conceal what is important, the false bottoms of the boxes, the use of mirrors; when the audience knows how these illusions are accomplished, mystification and belief die. For those 'savvy' people who do come back, the show becomes an interesting display of skill rather than magic – like an atheist enjoying a High Pontifical Mass.

Conjuror after conjuror, in the form of successive Faith Answers, has captured audiences, promising miracles but performing only illusions. The patter and the illusion keep the spectators in a state of hope until they die and are replaced with a new generation.

It is not the tricks of one Faith Answer but the system of illusion itself that must be exposed to stop the parade.

The opposing goals of social groups and individuals invite the establishment of Faith Answers. The functioning of the human mind makes doubting uncomfortable and Belief a safe harbour. From that pleasant rut the intellectual can re-arrange his prejudices instead of doing any fresh thinking, and so the parade of Faith Illusionists continues – nude emperors clothed by man's fears and society's longing for unquestioned control.

2. History Without the Faith Answer

The state of man's knowledge and the developments in his science and technology now require an abandonment of the traditional supersession of Faith Answer certainties in favour of a continuous pragmatic revision of goals and solutions.

In man's history there have been a sufficient number of atheists, agnostics and pragmatists to show that man can manage mentally without gods, holy goals and sanctified methods. There have also been times when there was no ruling Faith, but these periods have been relatively short.

The absence of 'permanent' criteria for action would at least remove an impediment to balance and perspective in choice. It was the existence of Hitler's racial Faith Answer that made it possible, even necessary for SS camp attendants to act as they did. Remove their belief in the Fuehrer's infallibility and the eternal verity of his great ends, and they might well rub their eyes in horror at what they had done.

This does not mean that individuals and groups could not act terribly in the absence of a Faith certainty. A lynch mob, borrowing the sadism and the paranoia of individuals, may from time to time excrete its madness. But without a justifying Faith, it must vanish after the act – its limited end achieved. But the Faith Answer's ends are unattainable; so long as their power lasts, the lynch mob remains convoked.

If a wand of disbelief could have touched the executors of Stalin's collectivization programme, more than seven million peasants would have lived on, their 'petty' lives suddenly assuming some importance in the absence of Faith.[3] Without the opposing Faith certainties of Hitler and Stalin, thirty million lives might have reached a more natural termination. And this sort of agony continues back through so much of human

[3] The figure of seven million is very probably low. Both Robert Conquest in *The Great Terror* and Gil Elliot in *The Twentieth Century Book of the Dead* give substantially higher estimates.

history with gods of one side backing their worshippers and gods of the other helping theirs. Homer's story of Troy is full of scheming gods and bloody humans. If the Trojan War or any other war were stripped of its 'heavenly' support – or its appeal to some sort of rationalizing scripture, it would be much more difficult to carry on.

Take away the issue of Communism from the Vietnam War and what could the sides have said? After all, the United States claimed it entered this war to prevent the spread of Communism; North Vietnam to carry the great message to the South. What can they say when the Faith Answer issue is destroyed? Who would want to make such sacrifices for just plain grubby greed? And if people were willing to take risks, they would be calculated on the basis of rewards offered, not for Great Faith Causes. Even when warfare was relatively cheap, and good, paying jobs hard to find, Kings often had to abandon their greedy aggressions simply because they couldn't afford to pay their mercenaries. In the 20th-century, with all the competition from less dangerous activities, the paying and finding of mercenaries would certainly be a limiting factor in war-planning, even without the super-bomb.

A 'Faith-thief' game can be played with history. What if the great and weighty Faiths of the high and mighty participants were abruptly dissolved? Assuming that the crucifixion of Jesus Christ was an historical event,[4] what would have happened during his interview with Pontius Pilate and the chief priests if they suddenly lost their Faiths? Pilate, the pragmatist, couldn't see any reason for killing Jesus except to have peace and quiet in the Jewish community; the priests, without Faith in their line of rightness, could have had no life and death quarrel with him and, of course, Jesus without his own Faith could have no more than a gentle ethic to offer. So, no crucifixion, no resurrection; nothing would remain except perhaps a few innocuously pleasant homilies.

This would have been 'good news' to the people to be labelled as heretics by the Holy Church and 'bad news' for the art lovers of later centuries. But it is also possible that art, divorced from the iconographical importunities of Christianity,

[4] There being no independent record or non-partisan confirmation of the existence of Jesus Christ, history is left to weigh secondary evidence. The weight of probability seems to be on the side of his existence; however, the holy and miraculous clothing of his life and dearth of biographical details do nothing to reassure the uncertain.

might have still decorated time with some worthwhile genre pieces. Science, instead of being crushed by the shortcut of revelation, might have made itself useful. Surely the ancient Egyptians could have found sounder public works than colossal stone homes for one or two dead bodies. And so it goes throughout history; man, by not facing himself and his personal and group dilemma, has spent lives and substance pretending to the knowledge and worship of various forms of the same illusion; that somehow something changeless has been found to which all lives and substance should be dedicated.

3. Exit Faith, Enter Pragmatism

It appears that in the third century BC a Greek scientist possibly Ctesibius of Alexandria, invented a steam-jet-reaction-engine. A few years later, Eratosthenes very closely approximated the earth's circumference. In the same century, Aristarchus of Samos affirmed and developed the Heliocentric Theory. Hydraulics, statics and mathematics made major advances in the 3rd-century BC. Houses were heated by the warm-air hypocaust-system, baths and sanitary plumbing were highly elaborated. All these scientific developments took place during a brief 'window of opportunity' provided by the absence of politically enshrined Faith Systems.

Then, bit by bit, a curtain was lowered over both technology and scientific speculation. All this waited in the wings to be rediscovered almost two thousand years later.

People may be unhappy at the thought of a world without Great Faith Answers but, it should be pointed out, even after the Ptolemaic System[5] and the old Creation Story were overthrown, life for most people continued normally. Human beings manage to adapt to reality. Man can even live with cosmic theories involving periodic obliteration, transformation and re-emergence. After all, at this moment he also lives with the certain knowledge of his own death. Why can he not live and function without the nudging of some transcendent Faith, distorting reality and stealing from his sense autonomy?

The destruction of the Faith Answer without replacement

[5] Claudius Ptolemaeus (c. AD 85-165) is credited with the detailing of an Earth-centred cosmos. The creation story seemed to bear this out and the Christian Church adopted geocentricity. Chart Nos 40, 44, 46.

would force man to examine degrees of sociality and parameters of individual freedom without reference to any doctrinal rigidity. No *Deus ex Machina* would descend to straighten things out. The work would proceed in the absence of Faith criteria, in the low heat of pragmatism, and be tempered by admitting the presence of paradox and the constant dynamic of change. The result would never be 'perfect', but no one would expect, demand, or even claim to know what perfection was. The advantage of this low-heat effect is that it admits the unobtainableness of perfection and so desanctifies all means for its attainment.

What might the practical effect of this 'outburst' of pragmatism be? Certainly there would be a much greater effort to balance society's aims with the means to be used in their attainment. Vague and high-flown sounding abstractions would have to be abandoned or translated into specific programmes. Speeches promising happiness, health, freedom, and a 'better life' have frequently been made by public leaders, and usually receive a good reception because the listeners imagine congenial means. Pragmatic audiences would want to know 'how'. For them, the 'what' would be contained in the 'how'. Leaders would find it difficult to obtain support without specifics. 'Do-able projects with limited objectives would be put forward rather than all-encompassing recipes for perfection.

No 'Higher Power' to save him.

The first named architect in history, Im-hotep, designed this, and quite probably believed in its purpose.

The directors of Topf und Söhn knew what this was for and let the Nazi Faith Answer rationalize its purpose.

134

Chapter Ten
CHOICE

Without the imposed objective criteria of a Faith System, man must learn to choose for himself. By eliminating – 'stripping away' – the learnt superstitions of his society, he will open the way to more intentional, less reflexive decision making.

1. The Mechanics of Choice

2. Stripping

3. Replacement

4. Testing and Resistance

5. Rut Resisting

At some far-off moment the human brain developed beyond being a storer of useful knowledge and experience and became conscious of its own consciousness. This transcendent act of self-discovery, together with its corollary 'the conceptualization of death', may well have been the catalyst that set human society on its triumphant path toward world domination.

'Awakening' in the world conscious, man cannot tolerate the idea that this consciousness, and hence his own existence, is meaningless. Since it has been impossible to prove the absolute validity of any set of Faith Beliefs (except, of course, to the Faithful), the proponents have, unconsciously and, at times, consciously, had recourse to a second line of defence – to make them 'seem' to be true.[1] As one individual seeks to convince another of his point of view, so the men of Faith attempt to create a consensus of meaning within Church, State or even the World. Christian, pre-1990 Marxism, and other missionary movements can be substantially explained in this light. If all men can be 'brought to agreement' or, at least, the opposition silenced, then existence can be firmly stamped with the meaningfulness of the 'Faith of the Day'. Dissent, under such circumstances, must be suppressed. It is not welcome in any society because it acts to destroy the current social consensus, endangering fundamental societal assumptions; but in a fully-

[1] This does not mean that the 'priests' of some Faith Answer, disbelieving in the central core idea, go about tricking their parishioners. Quite the reverse. It is because they do believe profoundly that they are willing to allow the faithful to believe in 'useful' forgeries, manipulated 'facts', dubious relics and questionable miracles. These are only a means to a 'great and true' end.

fledged Faith Answer society it is anathema.

Through its questions dissent raises the risk of meaninglessness. No wonder Catholics maintained their Inquisition and the Soviet Russians their 'special hospitals' for dissenters. They could not permit questioning. They had answers, but only to their own questions. Still, despite the falsity of those questions and the often cruel enforcement systems, Faith Answers have stood between man and his existential dilemma. They have provided a sanctified social fiction from which may be deduced 'desirable', 'meaningful' choice. Without this there would be nothing between man and the risk of meaninglessness. Without these systems of certainty he would have to order his own priorities against the axis of his life expectancy. He would have to ask himself 'How long have I got? And what do I want to do with that time?' In other words, he would have to learn to choose for himself.

While the cosmos can be seen to continue after each individual's death,[2] its continuing meaning to that individual has vanished. In the same way, an individual's death relative to that individual is a catastrophe to which he can attach no valid meaning. It is rather his life which he may safely endow with meaning. The values given to existence may be derived tenth-hand from parents, charismatic strangers, pop-song lyrics, or directly from a Faith Answer litany, but it is still the individual who decides, whether consciously or unconsciously, which values to accept, reject, or even create.

Individuals living through strong Faith Answer periods are informed bluntly as to what is right and what is wrong – down to often ridiculous details. When the Faith System is overthrown or loses its power to enforce, was that catechism of rights and wrongs correct? A new Faith System moves into the old one's power vacuum dictating an entirely new catechism. How could it have been a 'holy' mission in the Nazi world to kill Jews and Soviet Commissars in 1944, and a hanging offence only a year later? The Chief Inspector of Concentration Camps around that time found his meaning very simply. On his letterhead Teodor Eike emplaced, 'There is only one thing that is valid, <u>orders</u>!'

[2] In the case of severe mental deterioration, such meaning may have been lost well before the death of the body.

On this dust-speck of a planet the crossing of a few centimetres of boundary line can alter right and wrong drastically. On the Soviet Russian side clandestine 'factory' owners were once shot for the sin of capitalism; on the Turkish side, they might have been 'distinguished' citizens.

In 1985 on the Soviet Russian side of the Iranian frontier, a man writes a carefully-reasoned paper on Mohammed's unique ability to communicate with Allah in his dreams and then put the results in the Koran. The Soviet scholar observed that this way Mohammed easily settled the previous day's ecclesiastical arguments. The paper receives a prize. Bemused by a celebratory vodka, the scholar strays across the frontier and is promptly shot by order of the local Moslem clergy. Both the Soviet Union and the Iran of Khomeini were in possession of the 'truth' at the same time, except that it was totally contradictory, Communism knowing that there was no god and the Ayatollah knowing that he was 'His' personal representative on Earth.

Man has become used to 'differences of opinion' as the world has become, geographically speaking, more accessible. But Faith Answers are not talking about differences of opinion; they deal in absolutes 'worthy' of the giving or the taking of life. They 'know' they are right. Each announces the others' invalidity.

Suppose it were feasible to reduce all the great Faith Systems and the less-systematized Faiths to some kind of monster equation; there would be Shintoists, Marxists, Moslems, Buddhists, Nazis, Aztecs, Neo-Platonists, Moonies, as well as the conflicting sects of Christianity, of Islam, of Buddhism, and innumerable others all at odds with each other. The equation would be incredibly complex to write but, solved, it would add up to zero – the competing claims annihilating one another. Perhaps it is the difficulty man has experienced in 'writing' such an equation that has kept him from drawing the otherwise obvious conclusion: that manmade Faith absolutes exist only in the minds of the believers, and that is why, like any paranoic, they often become violent in the spreading and defence of their *idée fixe*.

If Faith Answers with their lists of rights and wrongs are overthrown by disbelief, where will individuals find a shibboleth, a measure to judge one path of conduct from another, or choose 'correctly' from an endless array of conflicting possibilities? When Alice in Wonderland, under threat of death, told the Queen and her court that they were 'nothing but a pack of cards', they collapsed and Alice could leave the land of marvels unharmed. So when man reduces Faith Answers and their wonder-working formulae to the level of Lewis Carroll or Hans Christian Andersen fairy tales, he will find himself outside the world of Faith Answer fantasy, and its ready-made meanings. Abandoning Faith's rubber-stamp value-system, the individual will have to find his own meanings. Choice, and the ability to confer meaningfulness would then be his responsibility.

Despite the massive conflicting literature on the source of meaning, the problem is not nearly as complex as has been imagined. Years of meditation on the ineffable, the One and the Many, subtleties of Talmudic interpretation, why the Buddha didn't answer certain questions, whether the Holy Trinity is one substance, are tangents leading off away from the searchers own existence; in a way, toys of the mind rather than tools for the uncovering of relevant meaning. In the desperate search for absolutes the searcher literally loses his self. If he abandons this kindergarten of diversionary thought with its sometimes disastrous impulses to act, the searcher can, at last, begin to accept himself as the ultimate source of meaning.

The bed-rock of individual meaning is the continuing existential requirement of the body's life-support system. This system 'knows' no doubts, it is life-oriented; it dies struggling to live. It goes about its complex tasks, periodically requiring conscious cooperation, signalling the time for eating, sleeping, defecating, warning of danger. Because each individual possesses a basically similar but qualitatively enormously different sensing-structure and vastly disparate abilities, he absorbs and collates both knowledge and experience differently, and his response to his system's requirements is unique. Since all Faith Answers are social engines of conformity, of mass human response and, consequently, enemies of individual choice, they are at war with the fundamental facts of human difference.

Faith Answers are 'after' a homogeneous society. They can never have it, or even the appearance of it, without restricting and, in a sense, imprisoning the sense-intake of individuals caught within it. When Jesus Christ is quoted in the Bible as saying 'Take no thought for the morrow, saying, what shall we eat? or what shall we drink? or, wherewithal shall we be clothed?... your Heavenly Father knoweth that ye have need of all these things...',[3] the way was opened for the Church to decide for its congregation what it was to eat, drink and wear. The Russian police raid on the Leningrad rock-record black market in 1980 occurred primarily because the Faith Answer in power wanted to decide to what music its citizens listened, as well as how they obtained it. In such situations profound private disbelief may be the only way to protect the self from these planned assaults on the senses.

1. The Mechanics of Choice

Once the primordial individual life-needs are satisfied – food, adequate clothing, protection from the elements – the simplest alternatives of choice present themselves. In Auschwitz, at a sub-level of subsistence, no one rejected shoes, clothing or food because of its poor quality. No one was finicky! Only above the lowest degree of the camp's pecking order would choice begin. Once liberated from mere subsistence, choice moves rapidly toward such complexity that its primitive roots tend to be forgotten.

Earlier choices combine to influence new ones determining to a great extent what a person will do in the future until, at last, in view of diminishing capacity to act, all choice, beyond life-needs, disappears.

During the period of capacity and opportunity individuals must build a frame of their own for judging choice, so that within the elective possibilities reigning at any particular historical moment, choice will belong to them, not to Faith's or tradition's pre-programming department. To do this effective-

[3] New Testament, Matthew 6, 31-32 (King James).

ly means the maximum possible removal of trained-in superstition and ritual conduct.

2. **Stripping**

It is easier by far to identify those parts of conduct that have
been openly rewarded and punished, as well as to alter such
patterns consciously. In stripping away conditioned elements
of behaviour however, the non-intentional, socially and
parentally-conditioned elements of an individual's choice pat-
tern, are probably more influential than the intentional. Simple
copying accounts for a substantial part of human behaviour.
This unconscious traditionalism is often hard to expose. Even
in the case of a whole society which thought itself to be
absolutely new – for example 'new-born' Marxist Russia –
there was, after the briefest of 'honeymoons', a simple continuance of Czarist society's traditional geopolitical aims as well
as the worst of its oppressiveness.

Freud's initiative in examining the unconscious layering of
the personality was important, but his almost religious fasci-
nation with sexuality, as the touchstone of psychoanalysis,
kept him from seeing the sexual repression of his time as only
one of the many socially-conditioned factors damaging comfortable personality development and, in extreme cases, induc-
ing neurosis. That sexual repression together with its resulting
neuroses could be only a manifestation of a temporary social
attitude he never understood. For him, his key of sexuality
unlocked all doors and so he based his theories on a social
symptom, not a cause. He was blinded by certainty.

Stripping this trained-in layering away is not always a pleasant activity; it involves questioning the gods and demons of
childhood and, at the same time, holding off their substitutes.
The 1960s in the West saw the children of generally 'comfortably off' parents hard at work questioning practically all their
trained-in values, and then often falling into the 'Marcusian'
New Left trap of freshened-up Marxism. They merely substituted one cliche ordered life for another.

'Tear down and build anew' has, certainly, been a motto of

'modernity' with damaging aesthetic and social results. There are many social conventions that have not much more than accepted ritual to recommend them, but are not important enough to bother fighting; however, it is essential at least to question it all. The task really should be to examine a structure to see if it can be better utilized, albeit with many changes, or whether it really must come down.

Obtaining the kind of distance necessary to see one's own upbringing and peer-pressure in perspective is hardly easy, but even the attempt to do so is a major step toward liberating choice from the influence of superstition and the rigidity of social training. Doubting trained-in values and systems of conduct will soon yield a copious crop of absurdities. The doubter will always find grist for his doubting. Nothing will ever be the same again.

3. Replacement

One of the conveniences of the Faith Answer is that it prescribes the 'correct' choice under practically all conditions. But how is it that considering the immense differences existing between people, and the infinity of choice, someone or some organized entity 'knows' what is best for an individual, and exactly how that person should behave?

Shouldn't such a preposterous pretension alert all 'intelligent' people to descry this as nonsense? It would be unwise to expect such a reaction from intelligent people. They are, in fact, in great demand, elaborating and maintaining those very restrictive systems. They are 'on the take!' Unless intelligent people obtain sufficient perspective to think outside the current social enthusiasm they will descry nothing – rather, they will help rationalize and systematize absurdity. Look at all the high-I.Q. lackeys who surrounded Hitler. Even considering the mixed bag the Allies put on trial in Nuremberg, the average I.Q. was 127.6. Their intelligence was dedicated to trying to make Hitler's horrendous fantasy come true. Of the ones still in power not one of them, until approximately a month before military defeat, made any effort to undermine that human nightmare.

Ever since the American and French Revolutions, 'freedom' and 'liberty' have been catch-words of almost anyone or any system seeking power. It has been the responsibility of 'intelligent' people to re-define freedom and liberty so that those fashionable words could be applied to the political system in power – or seeking power. Unless intelligence is possessed of perspective, freed from the mental claustrophobia of holy absolutes, it will simply assist in the construction of more effective means to limit individual choice.

One of society's techniques for holding down individuals is to accuse them of being imperfect. Judaism, Buddhism, Christianity, Islam and Marxism all tax individuals with this flaw. And, like quack doctors inventing a terminal complaint, claim to have a life-saving cure. It is not surprising, therefore, that individuals, imbued from childhood with the guilt of their gross imperfection and their need to follow some Faith Answer's self-improvement formula, may be shocked to be told that they themselves should be the best judge of what is best for them. If anyone thinks this is presumptuous, how does it compare with the pretensions of someone who wrote his book or preached sermons 145 years ago (Marx), or 1,365 (Mohammed), or 1,965 (Jesus), or even 2,500-2,600 (Buddha)? Someone 'who doesn't know you – who's never been introduced' tells you what you are to like, how to live your life, and whose Mafia-like organization is at your elbow ready to enforce its rules down to the smallest nit-picking detail. Which is more presumptuous?

Here are Alice's 'pack of cards', and 'the Emperor's New Clothes' combined; products of trained-in individual humility and the presumptuousness of the Faith Answer. The 'pack of cards' threatens, and 'the Emperor's New Clothes' announces the latest Faith Fashions, while individuals, cowed by devices like 'original sin', 'reincarnation', and tempted by 'resurrection', 'escape from pain', 'racial and economic perfection' obey. But whom do they obey?

At one time man invented gods who were part animal, nightmarish, weird, terrifying, unearthly-looking deities so awful as to command obedience; then, in a blow to imaginative sculpture, came the anthropomorphic, miracle-working gods of the Greco-Roman pantheon. They tended to be worshipped rather than obeyed – nobody except the State seemed to know what they wanted! Next came the God-man, of whom Jesus Christ was the most successful representative (there being many others). Upon the few maxims, miracles and parables of Jesus, one of the most pervasively suffocating societies was constructed by the Catholic and Greek Orthodox churches, adding to and reinterpreting doctrine as they felt necessary.

Jesus, up to the present time, has been the most successful 'flesh and blood' god on Earth.

The next era was the era of god's representatives with Mohammed at the head and the Popes a close runner-up. After centuries of heaven-inspired doctrinal manipulation to suit the political exigencies of the day, Marx and Hitler wrote books that factored god out of the political equation. Now man could take orders from man without recourse to God's intermediaries. Although man had replaced god, had even dropped the mask of representing him, he still expected total obedience in mind and body just as before. But this is now a 'magic' trick without sleight of hand; a rope trick without the rope. Considering the extent of this presumption, it seems almost an exercise in humility for individuals to 'prescribe for themselves!'

'But', asks a sceptic, 'Can man be trusted to choose for himself?' Perhaps the best answer to this is another question: 'Can Faith Answers be trusted any longer to choose for man?' Their 5,000-year-old history is a record of human wastage. And in view of their worsening 20th-century record, who should trust their personal future to more Stalins, Hitlers, Khomeinis, and Maos? When an individual makes mistakes the damage is limited. But when the 'Nazis' of the future 'err' there may be no one left to count the holocaust.

The sceptic persists: 'Man is totally inexperienced, he doesn't know how to choose for himself.' Again, the best reply may be a paradoxical question: 'Has man any other choice?'

The departure of Faith Answers from their formerly

enshrined position of dictators, of group and individual choice need provoke no anarchy. Human beings already have a value-analysis system which, working unimpeded by transcendent interference, can produce results that intimately relate to each individual: the mind's reaction to the messages of the senses released from Faith's hocus-pocus is more than capable of filling the 'power vacuum'. Nor would 'civilization' collapse.

It is man's social existence that provides individuals with choices that would otherwise be unavailable. Motion pictures, television, books, long-distance travel, etc., would be completely impossible without very intricate social cooperation. Nor would everyone have to be a full-time 'philosopher king' to deal with the complexities of existence. The world is full of ethical suggestions for organizing moral choice. Once these are cleansed of their change-impervious absolutes they might have some things of value to offer. For example, doing 'unto others as ye would they should do unto you' seems like a workable suggestion.

The form or kind of activity that people choose or have chosen for them always has some sort of behaviour criteria and more or less elaborated ways of judging success or failure.

The clearest example occurs in sports where there are detailed rules, umpires to observe the players and enforce the regulations. It is easy to see who plays 'clean', who 'dirty' and then to compare the quality of the players. The spectators not only go to see the skill of the players, but, perhaps, unconsciously, to be, at least for a short time, in a place where clear-cut values, rewards and punishments prevail.

For those immersed in the 'form' of the sport there arise few disturbing questions because the 'goals' are clear. Other activities may be equally or more exigent, like the experimental sciences, engineering, law or medicine. But those, being closer to the *materia prima* of human existence, may indeed raise disturbing questions, unless the scientist, engineer, lawyer or doctor so immerses himself in the discipline of the form that the ultimate results of his activities are of no interest to him. He has succeeded in what he was assigned to do and that is all that matters.

Because sports and games are an agreed fiction they seldom have any transcendental importance. No atomic bomb, pace-maker, micro-chip, or geodesic dome will emerge from the best of football games. The game is an end in itself. The players have little reason to study the end result of their activity since it can be seen on the scoreboard.

In 1953 when the nuclear physicist Robert Oppenheimer, who had been in charge of the atomic bomb project in Los Alamos, objected to the development of the hydrogen bomb, he was declared a 'security risk'. He had looked beyond his immediate activity – nuclear physics – and seen what society was planning to do with his 'success'. Unknown to the U.S security services at the time, Oppenheimer's 'weltenschauung' had, since the beginning of the project been covertly, extended to keeping the then Soviet Union fully informed of all technical developments in his field; meanwhile, the small fish spies, the Rosenbergs, were 'fried' in the electric chair!

It is less disturbing as well as superficially safer to bury one-self inside the chosen form, drawing from its ready-made rules a convenient code of mini-right and wrong. Outside there may rage Faith pogroms, revolution, *coups d'état, coups de palais, coups de main,* but in all cases, buildings must eventually be built or rebuilt, and so an architect may continue to ply his trade for whatever patron if he only considers the rights and wrongs of satisfactory design.

In the 28th-century BC, Im-hotep, the first architect known by name, built the Step Pyramid of Saqqarah for the Egyptian pharaoh, Djoser. It is extremely doubtful if he wondered whether he was wasting material and labour resources on this enormous burial place for his patron, resources that could be employed in favour of the living who needed homes during their lifetimes.

In 1941-42, a German engineering firm named Topf und Söhn in Erfurt bid successfully on some high-yield industrial kilns to be operated in the open air. The specifications were, to say the least, unusual. In fact, they really would not have been of any use except for the burning of human beings. This company's talented designers came up with a 'good' product at the 'right' price, and so their company 'succeeded' where others 'failed'. If the reader believes in Hitler's racial perfectionism, then the quote marks come off the value terms – good, right, succeeded, and failed – because within the context of the Nazi Faith Answer, Topf und Söhn were doing a 'fine', 'loyal' job, producing an excellent oven at a price that not only satisfied the German government, but apparently the company's stock-holders as well.

One of Topf und Söhn's engineers, who had adopted design engineering as his total self-absorbing life-form, could have truly been proud of his successful 'creation' without being in any way a National Socialist, and as long as he refused to be distressed by the ultimate use of his oven. If this 'sample' engineer had been a secret communist, and the time was after the invasion of Russia (June 22, 1941), then, in all probability, he would seek transfer or do his best to avoid working on the contract – the hackles of 'decency' and 'civilized morality' obtruding on his 'duty' to the company and Germany. He would not have believed or, if he had, he would have found ways to condone, the Soviet massacre of Polish officers in the Katyn Forest, discovered by the German invading Army in 1943. Where had he hidden this 'civilized morality when Stalin killed millions of simple peasants 'collectivizing' them? Suppose this 'sample' engineer were a sincere, practising Catholic; how would he have reacted? 'Disgust, moral indignation, extreme repulsion, the clear violation of all Christian principles' – yes, but where were those 'principles' in the powerful Catholic past? What happened to them during the Albigensian 'Crusade'[4] when the Pope sent his blessings on a 'Holy' War against other Christians; or the Fourth Crusade that plundered and raped Constantinople in 1204,[5] a city of 'brother' Christians? What about the organized torturings and judicial murders of the 'Holy' Inquisition? It seems that 'Holy' principles are adjustable. They are certainly no guarantee of 'civilized morality'.

[4] There being no independent record or non-partisan confirmation of the existence of Jesus Christ, history is left to weigh secondary evidence. The weight of probability seems to be on the side of his existence; however, the holy and miraculous clothing of his life and dearth of biographical details do nothing to reassure the uncertain.

[5] Claudius Ptolemaeus (c. AD 85-165) is credited with the detailing of an Earth-centred cosmos. The creation story seemed to bear this out and the Christian Church adopted geocentricity. Chart Nos 40, 44, 46.

4. **Testing and Resistance**

What would the 'stripped man' do at Topf and Söhn, assuming that he had compelling reasons for remaining in Germany? First, he could not doubt that Nazism was a Faith Answer and therefore capable of justifying abhorrent means for attaining its unattainable, transcendent objectives. Second: although the stripped man would try to excel in whatever he did (since mediocrity and tepidness hardly lead to the sense expansion he seeks), he would never be so deeply inside the chosen form (in this case design-engineering with a specialty in high-heat furnaces), that he would be oblivious to the results of his activities. Applying the stripped man's test, 'Is this a sense-expanding or contracting experience?' (leading away from Faith's prison and toward individual choice) – it would be hard to find grounds for believing that facilitating the extermination of human beings in the service of racial 'perfection' could lead to anything more than personal sense contraction. If the Faith Answer were successful in imposing its will on the world, that will would also be imposed on the stripped man; at least he would have his set of existential choices reduced, probably severely. Even if he had come up with a totally new and revolutionary way of cremating the human body and thereby receiving a clandestine medal from, and perhaps even dining at the Berghof[6] with, the then most powerful man in the world, this apparently 'on-going' expansive experience would certainly be leading toward an eventual contraction of his own choice possibilities. With hindsight such a contraction would be obvious because of the coming historical nemesis for those involved in the Holocaust, but even in the case of a Nazi victory, the areas of choice would have been further reduced. The more important a person is within a Faith System, the more time and energy that person must devote to it, unless it is in decline. People become enmeshed, exchanging their identity for that of the Faith's – they 'lead a life of devotion', and lives of devotion are rigidly devoid of choice.

Although the stripped man's values are subjective, exclusively based on the way things relate to him, whether or not

[6] Dining as a guest of Adolph Hitler would, within the Nazi context, have been a great honour; however, it is universally agreed by all memoir-writing guests that the food, conversation and company were almost always boring. Both wits and gourmets avoided the Fuehrer's 'board'.

people or events act to expand or contract his field of choice, he knows that it is the variegation of society that expands possibility, and monochromatic Faith Answers that contract choice. Burning a part of society for 'transcendental' reasons could not possibly be a path toward the increase of choice expanding transactions. Such a programme could only cut the cremators off from the potential social contributions of the exterminated. The only justification for such an activity would have been something like plague, where the lives of all were at risk.

The stripped man, especially with his connection to Topf und Söhn, would have heard that there were indeed, according to Reichsfuehrer Himmler (July 19, 1942), risks 'of contagion, both morally and physically' from the Jews and that 'total purification is necessary'. Hoess, commandant of Auschwitz, referring to the uses of Cyclon B gas, stated that 'we are now using it to destroy vermin in the camp.' With the advent of Hitler there was a deluge of anti-semitism, from the geneticist Lenz to the ravings of Julius Streicher in his grotesque magazine, *Der Sturmer*[7]. It was a highly contagious paranoia. This was where the real contagion lay – the real plague was the Nazi Faith Answer.

The stripped man trapped in Soviet Russia of the 1930s could easily have substituted 'Kulaks' – the rich peasants – for 'Jews', as Stalin's paranoic equivalents. He might have wondered how there could be so many millions of them; and all of them deserving a gruesome death. As an older Faith Answer than Nazism, Soviet leaders could already point to various Marxist heresies – Mensheviks, Trotskyites, Revisionists of all kinds. How would one not be caught up in all this exciting 'action-oriented' dialectic? And what, if anything, could the stripped man do about it?

With even less possibility of emigrating than from Germany he would have to stay doing whatever he could do to satisfy himself that wherever feasible he was damaging the 'Faith' with the least damage to his own scope of choice.

Some satisfaction is to be gained in fighting societies which have so reduced choice that there is hardly anything left but to attempt to undermine them.

[7] This magazine's pornographic assaults on world Jewry were sufficiently gross to cause its removal from news stands during the 1936 Olympic Games. Many Nazi leaders found it abhorrent, and some occasionally managed to have it banned within their particular jurisdictions.

Even the assumption that there might have existed a stripped man in some past societies may be extreme. How would anyone gain the perspective to re-examine his relation to and the truth of the society's adoptive Faith, if it permeated everything and everyone around him? If the Faith's saturation point is complete, all rival possibilities will be unknown or, if known, distorted to an absurd extent and shut out. In these cases the energy of instinctive dissent may have to content itself with espousing heresies, battening onto aspects of the Faith that are controversial, or, *in extremis,* becoming a Satanist in the Middle Ages or a capitalist in the Old Soviet Union.

It may be that it is only now that a truly stripped man may emerge. The world has seen such an historic telescoping of religio-social movements since the French Revolution; such 'golden' impossible promises swallowed by generation after generation of idealist zealots all doomed, and dooming themselves and the rest of the world to catastrophic disappointments. One 20th-century individual could have seen the jingoistic madness of the First World War, followed by the international hopes for the 'miracle of the Russian Revolution' and its ideals, the punctual trains of Mussolini, Hitler's German consciousness-raising operation, the miracle of Mao's Red Book, the wonder wrought by Islam's revival in Iran, and mini-cults like Jones's, Manson's, Koresh's, Luc Jouret's, and Shoko Asahara's Aum Shinri Kyo, 'Supreme Truth'.

Like the 5,000-year-old man, no one could have believed in all of this. So, perhaps, seeing how the 20th-century dealt with ideals might serve as a science-non-fiction laboratory for at least starting the stripping process. First World War patriots who died ridiculous deaths by the millions in trench warfare, or gaining a few kilometres only to lose them again, were tragically wasted. Mussolini's Fascism linked up with old-fashioned imperialism terminated all its posturing grandiloquence with the grotesque hanging of the Great Dictator and mistress from the roof of a garage in Milan's Piazzale Loreto. The 'idealistic fruits' of the Russian Revolution ripened with multi-million deaths of the Kulaks, the Purge Trials, the Gulag Archipelago and the 'special-treatment' insane asylums, and then the spectacular collapse of the Soviet Union.

Those who followed Mao's mass hypnosis course, in which just short of a billion human beings were shoved into the same size 'ready-to-wear' clothing and ideals, were permitted to 'discover' that the Red Book worked no miracles, that Mao, himself, had 'feet of clay'; and then see his successors adopt a market-oriented economy complete with stock exchanges! The post Shah Islamic revival in Iran was greeted by all those who were 'in love with Faith' as automatically good. But the executions continued, the exalted faithful stalked the world in assassination squads and terror ruled Iran.

The 'mini' cults like Manson and Jim Jones are no more absurd than the 'maxi' Faith Answers. Usually society has no trouble dubbing them with its most opprobrious terms. But, although they are terrible, they are too small to do massive harm, too easy to spot, and relatively simple to dismantle. Manson's 'family's' ritual killing of Sharon Tate can be no more justified than Robespierre's guillotining of the ancient Marechalle de Noailles, the massacre of Hitler's Jews, or Stalin's Kulaks. Just because someone has a 'bible' to slap and 'priests' to back him up does not turn murder into a dignified necessity. *Mein Kampf, Das Kapital*, the *Red Book*, Rousseau's *Contrat Social*, the *Holy Bible* have all been used to do exactly that – justify and dignify torture, murder and enslavement. All of this is part of the stripped man's study course to which he can add and arrange not only current events from daily papers (if he lives in a strong Faith Answer system, he will have to work harder at disentangling fact from propaganda), but empirical observations, as to how such things impinge on his life.

5. Rut Resisting

Where the full force of repressive systems does not prevail, the stripped man should also keep his own life-form under constant scrutiny to be sure that it does not lose its intentionality. The individual needs society to extend his range of sense experience and choice but must never forget that the group (even a small group) is still concerned with control of its individual members.

For the stripped man the nakedness of a Faith Answer's control is obvious. But there are other forms of group control that are less recognizable. Applause is one of them. Earlier it was said that 'people can literally be applauded to death'. On a lesser scale, 'success' and social acclamation can actually be responsible for a reduction in an individual's field of choice. The applause, the crowd-conferred feeling of rightness and importance, can carve a 'splendid' life-rut, create a gilded prison for the world's superstars, as well as for the relatively unknown 'successes'. In this manner an individual may be 'taken over' and manipulated by the group up to the point that he has (as is so frequently said) no private life, and lives in fear of failing to please.

'Successful' people who live within the form chosen by themselves or in some degree forced upon them, who have constructed for themselves no redoubts or perspective, no retreat for questioning, will be totally 'in hock' to their success, completely enslaved, enthralled by their employing group. When they no longer render the services demanded, they have no place to go, no stance on their own value, no formula for distinguishing the 'playing cards' that surround them.

They are as helpless as retired workers with no replacement interests.

The stripped man will be 'himself', not a plumber, farmer, computer designer, scientist, performer, philosopher, etc. His continuing search for widening and deepening his sense experience will to some extent always be at odds with the 'success' requirements of the form in which he works. This alone is sufficient to distance him from total absorption.

The more repetitive and boring the activity, the more important becomes the manner of using the funds at his disposition. (Again, it must be above minimum subsistence level, as in the concentration-camp example.) To the extent that it is used for the same things week after week, year after year, the deeper and deeper life-rut is carved, and the more difficult it becomes to clamber out.

Calling repetition and concentration within a life-form a 'splendid' rut, or just a rut, seems to imply pain for the individuals who live this way. While some may feel unfulfilled, most people, depending on the quality of their mental balance, probably find the rut's security sufficient compensation for the risky rewards and punishments awaiting them 'outside'.

It is in the nature of things to repeat successful repetitions until they no longer succeed, or until an aberrant offshoot is more successful. Then it too will be similarly repeated, until replaced.

People complain about the boring, repetitive work they do, but many of them, released for the day from that work proceed to use those free hours for repetitive, ritual 'recreational' activity: the same friends, the same bar, the format television show with minimal variations, approximately the same food, the same woman or man asking the same questions and getting the same answers and, very frequently, holidays in the same place. In this case there is a minimum of sense expansion. But it does not follow that people living in such a manner would be at all willing to undertake a re-appraisal of the composition of their life. For them the rut has important advantages. Fear is reduced, they 'know' where they are and, most fundamentally, they are already in the rut. Although they might not be willing to admit it, they are sufficiently content not to risk a change.

The stripped man may not be a Leonardo da Vinci, able to work well at almost anything. He may not be able to enter a socially-impressive profession, but that too may actually work in his favour – no clients to entertain, no after-hours competitiveness. When his work is over he may concentrate on increasing his sense experience: sound, music, taste, visual values, touch, the sensual delights of companionship; in this way the rut of his money-earning is more than compensated for by the way he spends the rest of his time.

The more he experiences the greater the amplitude of what he may be able to experience, assuming that he proceeds with an adequate sense of balance. He is building an inverted pyramid of increasingly complex inter-dependence and personal delight. He cannot be 'apolitical'. If he retires from the struggle to increase choice and maintain social exactions at a minimum, a new perfective scheme based on 'shiny' new absolutes might well emerge, leading to another era of enslavement.

The stripped man's path toward extending the range of his sense experience is not off towards some lone, Heideggerian existential mountain-crag, or a Nietzschean superman's Bavarian eyrie wasting his time testing 'the power of a will according to the amount of resistance it can offer and the amount of pain and torture it can endure...'[8]

Instead, the stripped man's path is straight back into a wary but active relationship with society from which he will not expect to obtain his values, but rather a more ample opportunity to choose his own.

With the departure of all absolutes from his life, the paradoxical constant 'change' excepted, his field of choice is limited only by the kind of society in which he lives, and the life-form or forms he adopts or into which he is forced by circumstances. Whatever decision he takes can have no absolute assurance of rightness or wrongness. But, since such absolutes are only man-made fictions, he has lost nothing except fallacious assistance in his choosing. Decisions with a touch of doubt attached are far less likely to damage other individuals than those conceived in transcendent certainty.

The stripped man understands the flaws of choice, but also the practical need to choose. His search for balance in choice will be without false reference to pre-digested answers. The physical life-requirements of the body, the major and minor pleasures of the senses, social interplay, the deepening of pleasure and enhancing of choice – judgement through 'feeding' the mind – these all act as guides to the construction of relative meanings fashioned to each individual's circumstances; certainly a far better fit than Faith's 'hand-me-downs'.

[8] Bertrand Russell in his *History of Western Philosophy* quotes this passage from Nietzsche. Russell, writing in the middle of the Second World War, has been criticized for exaggerating Nietzsche's influence on the growth of Nazism. Friedrich Nietzsche's ideas of racial aristocracy, his 'noble' Superman (Overman), 'who enjoys practising severity and harshness upon himself and feels reverence for all that is severe and harsh' ('What is Noble', *Beyond Good and Evil),* appealed most strongly to Adolf Hitler, who had his picture taken in the Weimer Nietzsche museum with the philosopher's bust—the attitude struck was one of adoration. Although Nietzsche repudiated anti-semitism, the race of 'magnificent blond brute(s) avidly rampant for spoil and victory' led by 'a particularly strong kind of man, most gifted in intellect and will' who would 'become lords of the earth' *(Will to Power)* hardly sounds like the short dark Jews of Eastern Europe.

154   An invasion to stay in office, cloaked in patriotism.

Chapter Eleven
A PRACTICAL CHOICE

Man should deal with man as he is, not as a creation of his fantasies. With the stripping away of socially-learnt ideas of how to live and what to do, man would be better able to tailor choice to his actual needs. By concentrating on the life that is, instead of sacrificing it for the immortality schemes of Faith Answers, individuals can have a fuller life.

A substantial part of this book has been devoted to pointing out the way in which Faith Answers and their dregs have terminated, impeded, blocked or redirected the personal development of individuals.

In the last chapter on choice, the engineer from Topf und Söhn was presented with a real, transcendent dilemma. Most individuals in Western society do not have to deal with such extreme situations. Their lives of risk are vicarious – on the screen and in books. For them the extremes of existence may be emotionally exciting or, as in this book, perhaps theoretically interesting; but unless those ideas can be applied to ordinary life, they will have little cogency for most people. In fact, a great part of all behaviour – ordinary life – in the Western world is still a conditioned mixture of the lees of Faith Answers and fashion.

This chapter and the next are particularly directed at readers who, without necessarily doing battle with the Faith Giants themselves, can profitably clear away those useless remains from their lives.

What are some of the conclusions drawn in the earlier chapters, and how might they be put to work?

First, man's dreams of after-lives, heavens, hells, warriors' immortality and all manner of post-mortem social awards should be recognized as human nonsense designed to create social 'braves' and lead social cowards into doing what they are told.

Second, individual death – *your* death – is, relative to you, catastrophic, and it is a waste of time, even a dangerous waste of time, to try and give it meaning. So concentrate on the life that is – give this meaning. Not a hand-me-down meaning, but one that has been personally tailored. One day man will conquer death, then there will be no need to give death meaning and the self-sacrificers of the past will seem absurd.

Third, it is essential to examine training inherited from home, friends, schooling, social media – preachers, parables on television, newspaper and magazine editorializing – and select what is personally useful, what makes sense. Here each individual must play the part of his own 'devil's' advocate, rigorously questioning all this 'inheritance' – the unconsciously-trained acceptance of current social customs and fashionable attitudes. Only then can man come to construct a society based on how man 'is', rather than on wish-fulfilment fantasies of how he might be perfected.

Unfortunately this programme can only be suggested in a general way because each individual is so different – far more different inside than out. A few milligrams of LSD for one person could be an expansive experience, for another it could be an unmitigated nightmare, and for a third person it could trigger a lengthy psychotic episode. This is why there is so much conformist propaganda to put everyone in the same 'fits-all' behaviour strait-jacket. 'Deep Faith' is the anaesthetic society uses to conceal the discomforts of being 'de-individualized'. It also serves to camouflage the Faith Answer's control machinery.

A deeply believing Soviet Marxist could not have accepted that the Old USSR's emigration laws, travel restrictions, and their enforcement constituted a diminution of personal freedom. The arguments advanced to justify such restrictions would almost certainly appear to non-believers as sophistic nonsense; but, they were good enough for believers. In Mrozek's play *Out at Sea,* Thin sums up the genre by saying that "True Freedom exists only in the place where there is no ordinary freedom'.

A country with a Faith Answer backing its rules has an easy time excusing oppression; it points to its god, its book. But where there is no such Faith gimmick, for example as in Nixon's Watergate 'cover-up' excuses can be unmasked. This may be why States seem to relish war. Once war has begun, the war itself is the control gimmick – a total justifier. It is always a 'just' and 'noble' war, but it is ironic that both sides are 'just' and 'noble' at the same time, until the alleged 'nobility' and 'justice' of the loser's is obliterated by the winner's.

For millennia States, tribes, cities and mercenaries have dashed off to war with ill-concealed whoops of joy. With the advent of atomic and biological warfare, States possessing these weapons have not wanted to risk their very existence by using them in what would appear to be a 'pot-lach' war of material and human devastation. There is no doubt that this has cooled interest in anything approaching, or even potentially approaching, a conflict on an international scale. But small States continue to ravage their neighbours in a grand, old, 'imperialistic' fashion, availing themselves of 'war powers' to regiment their peoples and stifle dissent.

The 1982 invasion of the Falkland Islands by Argentina is an almost perfect illustration of the point. A widely unpopular military 'Junta', beset by dissent, economic troubles and international inquiries into human rights' violations decided to invade islands continuously held by Britain for some 150 years. In a moment crowds were in the streets shouting approval. All Argentine school-children are taught that las Malvinas (the Falklands) belong to Argentina. At a blow the 'Junta' with its jingoistic pronouncements had eliminated strikes and all other manifestations of discontent. Nothing had improved for the 'disappeared people', the hungry, the jobless, the politically disenfranchised, except that the legerdemain of a popular war now anaesthetised opposition and converted disgust into patriotic fervour.

War's utility to the state is a gamble – very often a final all or nothing. Since wars can be lost, the advantages may be brief. The excuse of war or the risk of war is extended wherever possible to maintain 'war-time controls'. But a clear loss is a disaster; the 'Junta' in Argentina had all 'resigned' within 3 months of defeat and the internal chaos hidden by the war-time sacrifice emerged.

History with its endless dates, rising and falling of dynasties, conquests, blood-baths, heroes and villains of the moment is usually either learnt as an irrelevant jumble of difficult to remember events or taught as a proof of someone's deterministic theory. In the latter case history is much easier to follow because selected events are hung neatly on the skeleton of theory. Any happening that spoils the hypothesis is left out or reinterpreted to conform with it. This kind of simplification has been convenient enough to have been acceptable to all previously-known societies. According to Christianity*, all history awaited the birth of Jesus Christ. And for Marxists history, from the Middle Ages on, moved inevitably toward Marx's discovery and solution of social conflict. Of course, this is hindsight nonsense, but if wrapped up properly by priests and intellectual toadies, people accept it as 'gospel'.[1] Take away society's 'cover story' for decreeing what individuals should or should not do and man can look behind this screen.

This is not the 'total' path to finding the 'good life', but it is an essential first step. After this, the cloak hiding human power- struggles will be gone and man may get to know himself better. Those elements of the make-up of human beings that have been swept under the carpet by religious and quasi-religious fantasizing can be studied and subsequently fitted into social systems constructed on a base of how human beings actually are rather than according to someone's images of perfection.

For example, there are resemblances between human society and the 'barn-yard', especially in the establishment of a 'pecking order'. Where perhaps the cocks are ahead of their human equivalents is that they almost certainly do not know how to

* Melvyn Bragg, a well-known arts and moral discussion presenter (BBC Easter 1996) said *'Morality did not exist before Jesus Christ'*. This remark went unchallenged and presumably reflected a latent consensus.

[1] An interesting illustration of the work of 'intellectual' toadies combining with society's search for control is the glossing over by Marxist theoreticians of the failure of attempted revolution in advanced capitalist countries and the 'success' of revolution in 'backward' peasant societies, such as Russia, China, Cuba and some poor African nations – precisely the reverse of Marx's analysis. In such 'advanced' countries as Czechoslovakia inter alia, Stalin engineered 'revolutions' were maintained by Soviet military power. The tergiversations of Marxist theoreticians to explain these 'anomalies' (to their parishioners) were strongly reminiscent of the Catholic Church's attempts to justify geocentricity.

kid themselves or the other chickens as to why they fight to be head cock! Why not accept that power over our 'fellow' men is a driving force in human relations – part of the social instinct – highly developed in some people and dormant in others? Both Christianity and Marxism have pretended to find formulae to exorcize this power demon, so one discovers 'humble', life-abnegating monks hopping up on the papal throne and self-sworn commoners like Stalin clambering to absolute power over the bodies of the people.

Unless some form of mass lobotomy is practiced there is and will be no way to change this fundamental drive of man. But taking this fact of life into account a canny society may well be able to utilize it for the general welfare. Ancient Greek society used to give to its rich men at least a touch of political power in exchange for expensive public projects; the Romans too had an office especially designed for 'showoff' rich men. Greed for possessions kept the rags-to-riches 'successes' of the 19th-century 'burning the midnight oil' building an immense industrial society. Attempts in China under Mao Tse-Tung to eliminate greed for possessions (alias incentive) or power from Mao-Marxist society practically halted the Chinese economy and threw the State into a chaotic condition.

Man looks at his character, is dissatisfied and pretends he can change it – but the change is never more than plastic surgery which can only alter immediate and superficial appearances. When early Marxism's human face-lift removed the evil – 'property'– man fought bloodily for power; and if the United States of the latter half of the 20th-century made possessions and money paramount, paying and treating even minor corporate executives far better than generals, admirals, government administrators and even the President, why should anyone be surprised that some second-rate incompetents moved into the offices of national power? The United Kingdom enacted a national health scheme in 1947 which appealed to medical idealism. Due to its relatively poor salaries, it soon made every doctor a philanthropist. Gradually private practice increased and the quality of public health treatment decreased until in 1980 an engineering union shocked the Trades Union Council by announcing that thenceforth its members would receive private instead of public health treatment.

The liberal-humanitarian societies (for want of a better term) of the 20th-century doctrinairely insisted that human beings are good, kind and generous and that crime, cruelty and meanness derive from social conditions. This thesis is at first quite attractive because it practically eliminates individual guilt, throwing the blame on society in general. But then if society in general is guilty, who is left to punish its naughtiness? It seems that the answer, curiously enough, is that those very victims of bad social conditions in such liberal-humanitarian societies are the castigators-designate. Returning home after being robbed at pistol or knife-point or trussed up in a kidnapping, the robbed or the kidnapped can console themselves with the justice of the situation that the true victims are their robbers or kidnappers – victimized by social conditions – who now most properly chastise the society which failed them! The laws and the enforcement of such a guilt-ridden society will not act as a sufficient deterrent to crime.

All of these failure examples – the early Marxist attack on property, the United States's disincentives in the public sector, the United Kingdom's *de facto* effort to make doctors into philanthropists and the liberal-humanitarian society's plague of guilt – derive from doctrinaire views of what man is. Instead of harnessing man's 'crude' drives for the general benefit, these social views insist upon the reality of a fictitious man.

As was said in an earlier chapter, man may literally be applauded to death. This is the extreme risk, but themes like patriotism, being a good Christian, a good Communist, a good Moslem, even a good corporation-man are usually lower-key forms of the same thing – the group taking advantage of the individual's social instinct. 'Good' British patriots bought 3% government bonds in 1946 'to aid in the reconstruction of war-torn Britain', some redeemable as late as 1975. What with income taxation of the 3% return and the vast inflation experienced in Britain, it doesn't take an economist to see how those patriots were bilked. Disabled veterans forgotten in sparse 'economically-run' hospitals must, if they allow themselves the painful luxury, wonder how well their society has rewarded their sacrifice.

Individuals should always be alert to the group's 'smiling recruiting-sergeant' and the eternal invitation to sacrifice.

This discussion certainly is not a charter for hermits; they miss the most exciting and rewarding aspect of existence – interaction with other people. It is only a warning, an attempt to introduce criteria for judging group values and remaining an individual within group situations: 'What do they want of me?', 'Is joining or remaining in the group worthwhile for me?' These are serious questions that should be continually in the mind of anyone wishing to maintain individuality but still enjoy the social benefits of group-individual interaction. Someone may say the questions are too self-centred. Of course they are self-centred. That is part of viewing man as he is. If people asked questions like this and investigated groups before they 'invested' their selves they would not become organized 'playthings'.

Self-centredness is no evil. It is simply a fact. Individual difficulties arise where people pretend that they are 'supermen', 'saints', that the wearing of ideas has profoundly altered the wearer. All they have done is to cover-over how they are and so distort their understanding of themselves. It is relatively harmless to do this with clothing fashions, but wasteful and disastrous with Faith fashions.

Let us take a look (or should it be a half-embarrassed peep?) at how man really is. First of all, he is a dying animal physically battling to survive. His brain pooled with the rest of his species has made him the most powerful animal on earth. Without his social instinct none of this would have been possible; however, this very instinct has laid him open to participating in fatally misguided activities involving pointless aggressiveness and self-sacrifice. Various social systems have encouraged man, the individual, not to question: 'Theirs not to reason why; theirs but to do or die.' Only someone, who is willing to accept himself unadorned by social propaganda, willing to accept his self-centredness, can begin to reconstruct valid relationships between his individualism and his participation in groups. It is that very self-centredness, upon which the organs of society pour so much scorn, which can act to protect individuals.

In an earlier chapter it was said that there is no such thing as unselfishness – only the appearance of it. Human beings have no choice whatever but to act in such a way as will respond to the most exigent, most pressing, demands of the senses in concert with long or short-term requirements of their self-image. But this self-centredness, once admitted, is much less likely to lead to 'meanness', 'cruelty', and 'selfishness' than the self-deceptions of Faith Answers adepts, because it soon becomes clear that enlightened self-interest implies treating other people well. To put it unromantically, the gratification of one's social instinct requires kindly, friendly and affectionate behaviour toward others wherever possible. No one needs to believe that Jesus Christ is in Heaven to accept the Christian homily: '... as you wish that men would do to you, do so to them.'[2]

The eventual (objective) effect of enlightened self-interest may then be very similar to that obtained via certain Christian practices. But, and here the 'but' is vital, this has been obtained without the distortion of one's life – no catechism to memorize, no Inquisitions or religious wars, no religion-imposed rigidities. Marxism called attention to the mechanics of possible economic oppression, but then exalted a violent form of prohibiting such oppression into a totalitarian religion. For all the bits of utility that may be found in the Faith Answers of the world, there is a mass of absurdity which far outweighs the life-enhancing value of those bits.

[2] Luke 6, 31. In this case the Revised Standard Version of the Holy Bible is more effective than the King James edition: 'As you would that men should do to you, do ye also to them likewise.'

Galtieri is SACKED

GALTIERI: 'Resign or go to jail' he was told

NICOLAIDES: He takes over Galtieri's command

When the leaders' cloaks came off.

One toppled...

...another waiting.

Chapter Twelve
A NEW SOCIETY

The action of change on man-created systems of 'permanence' even-tually exposes their absurdity; but, with the new technologies of war and mind-control, there may be very little time left. Man cannot await events, he must abandon his love affair with Faith Answers, because in the next great Faith war, all may well be lost.
1. An Unhallowed World

If individuals begin to understand the machinery of Faith Answers then social power based on Faith would be under-mined, and a new kind of society could then emerge.

Once the transcendental justification through the Faith Answer has been removed, society could set about practical and useful activities. Earlier, the 'full life' of Heinrich Himmler was contrasted with the millions of deaths upon which his 'full life' depended. While Faith-freed individuals would insist that society as a whole make available to all people the best oppor-tunity possible for them to expand their 'acquaintance' with existence, society's corollary task would be to prevent such 'full' lives as Himmler's from being lived at the expense of oth-ers. This would mean that society would have to act as referee instead of Guru.

There would still be an important duty remaining to the social whole, at least as long as death is a fundamental fact of individual life. When the insouciant mistress of Louis XV reportedly said, *'Aprés nous le déluge,'* Madame de Pompadour spoke for all dying individuals especially those who have no Faith Answer or loved ones for whom they are willing to sac-rifice part or all of their present existence.

Removing the Faith Answer as continuing social glue means that self-sacrifice for a 'millennial' future, albeit illusory, would end. Unless the 'immortal' social whole acted to mitigate this Louis XV attitude, those presently alive might rob the unborn of their opportunity to expand their 'acquaintance' with existence. The immortal aspect of society gives it a different viewpoint from that of individuals, even though it is, paradoxically, made up of mortals.

With Faith and chauvinistic jargon removed, the potential of the social whole for immortality still exists. In fact, it may actually increase its potential by eliminating Faith wars. But, if that society permitted one generation to rob the next, there would, eventually, be no inheritance for it to pass on, and so it would be essential to establish a pragmatically based balance between what living individuals need now for their 'full life', versus what the next generation needs for its 'full life'.

With the intricate group-individuals interconnections that must be maintained to sustain a high-technology society, there will be no social need for transcendental gimmicks to maintain the cohesion of the social centre.

The social centre's function would be two-fold: first, providing a frame within which an individual would have the opportunity to explore and develop without preventing others from enjoying a similar opportunity. Second: it would serve as a source of continuity and balance between the living and the unborn so that one generation would not be permitted to rob another. Those living would not be required to make such sacrifices for the future as would seriously reduce their current 'full life' opportunities, nor would they be allowed to consume so much in the present that those to come would have substantially less opportunities for a 'full life'.

Without the overriding rationale of transcendent gimmickry, society is cut down to size, but because of technological necessity and man's inherent social drive, it is by no means emasculated. It would still carry out pragmatically useful projects – indeed, it would not be authorized to build more 'pyramids'.

The mediation of individual disputes and the provision for the future generations would be high among its other obligations and constitute an important part of its *raison d'être*. Of course, it would never achieve perfection, but, deprived of millenarian gods and goals, it would not be trying for perfection.

Society's job would be to maintain a triple balance. Firstly, between the competing 'full lives' of individuals; secondly, the needs of individuals versus the social centre's minimum requirements and, thirdly, a balance between the needs of the unborn and those presently alive.

In other words, society, to secure its own future would have to defend the interests of the unborn; but being composed of mortals it would be required not to 'tax' the living excessively.

This balance would never be static – rather a continuing series of dynamic adjustments made possible by accepting existence's fundamental feature – change – and the consequent rejection of transcendental systems of certainty.

In all history there has never been such an opportunity as man now has to construct criteria that have no Faith base, criteria that derive from the logic of individual existence, balanced by the survival needs of the social whole.

It is possible that the rise of man as the earth-dominating species was assisted by constant ritual associations which were rationalized by the imperative needs of an unending procession of cults. These nascent Faith Answers demanded a great deal of the adept's time, as they still do, but they may have also been useful in socializing wild individualists and autochthonous families into larger, more viable groupings, where, to some extent, the division of labour and skills could take place. However, now that man is, at this time, clearly the dominant species, Faith Answer societies are not only unnecessary but, as previously stated, actually threaten the survival of the species through ideologically rationalized warfare. The needs of Faith Answers are no longer relevant to what may once have been their function.

Paradoxically, human society, once threatened by biological and geophysical forces, may now be threatened by what may have been one of its tools of successful emergence – its super glue, the Faith Answer.

Individual survival is now so clearly dependent on the effective interlocking matrix of world technology that no Faith Answer glue is necessary to keep a society together.

It is again paradoxical that behavioural sciences are developing increasingly refined tools and techniques for forging social conformity just when they are least necessary and most dangerous. The risks involved are that a Faith Answer employing such techniques could maintain itself in power even at the cost of the survival of man. If the 'Reverend' Jim Jones of Guyana, or the 'Branch Davidian' Koresh had access to the 'war button', would they not have pushed it instead of passing out Flavour-Aid and cyanide? Or flammable spirits? The 1995 gassing of ordinary people in the Tokyo metro by the 'SupremeTruth', Aum Shinri Kyo cult is probably a foretaste of things to come. Can one assume as one checks one's daily paper that such a man as Hitler, quite prepared for a world version of Gotterdammerung, will never again emerge?

Beyond the avoidance of a universal cataclysm, what is to be gained is not a more powerful society, but a society whose power has been moderated by a consensus of disbelief in Faith absolutes, where individuals, relieved of the feudal exactions of this outmoded *ancien* Faith *régime,* can reemploy their sequestered senses for their own account. But recalling the dichotomy of objectives between individuals and groups, it isn't likely that this yoke will be freely lifted; the power will not be ceded lightly. Like burned-out ideamen desperate for their jobs, Faith Answers may well offer the world even more incredible Answers than cure-all economics, cure-all race, and 'new wave' crack-pot cults.

When a group or a society adds Faith to its control mechanism, the needs of each single part are suppressed or redirected in favour of the 'glorious whole', the principle being that as much will be taken from the parts as they *en masse* will permit. Consequently, when Faith Answers are in control, all potential islands of resistance are reduced to impotence or eliminated: the treatment of trade unions and news media under Communism and Fascism, Freemasonry under Catholicism; in fact, any group that is not dedicated to toadying to the established Faith Answer, is subject to reduction. Without the rationalizing 'super truth', the paranoic centripetalism of the group monolith is no more, and the parts are freed to be alone or to form groups with pragmatic rather than transcendent goals. Within this context, individuals would be free up to the limits of interpersonal toleration to explore and expand their subjective existence without the exactions and pressure of a 'super truth' or the extravagant promises of another 'waiting in the wings'.

On hearing this proposal, all kinds of reflexive thinking is triggered: is it anarchy? Counter-revolution? For some, Faith is all they believe they have. But after the Faith dust has settled and the reflexive outrage cooled, the non-affiliated intelligence may see it as a chance for individuals to develop themselves within the minimum necessary organizational context. It is unsanctified government forced to explain itself in pragmatic terms without references to any sort of scripture. *It is iconoclastic but not anarchic.*

Anarchy is a socially regressive idea, since it points toward an antique state of nature, successfully rejected during the evolution of the human species. Individual expansion requires group interplay and assistance to protect and build an increasingly challenging matrix in relation to and within which individual subjective existence may be amplified. Understanding the dangers to the individual as well as the necessity and utility to him of the group, should enable him to avoid its paranoic schemes, but participate in its benefits.

1. **An Unhallowed World**

Those who manage to tolerate the absence of absolutes, refusing the facile comforts of a Faith Answer, will enjoy certain benefits. Their existence need not be a mad hedonistic romp coupled with knowing moments of stoical tristesse. Their lives will be more intentional, their decisions less automatic. They will be both in and outside a situation simultaneously, and so incapable of either giving or obeying blind orders. They would be poor army material. In their hands, group objectives would be viewed pragmatically and so subject to revision. Means to obtain such pragmatic ends would have to match the ends – unlike transcendent ends which rationalize any and all means. With society robbed of its grand illusions, the machinery would be stripped of its former finery, unhallowed and exposed.

The ancient Israelites were well-advised to hide the Ark of the Covenant within the 'Holy of Holies' and spread tales of dead desecrators (very holy things don't seem to improve on close inspection). The governance by divine right of kings has disappeared – the 'divine' right of governments to rule through Faith Answers is just as absurd: when Robespierre got up in the morning he invariably 'knew' what the people wanted. He didn't need to ask them, and he certainly didn't.

Whatever politico-economic structures might emerge from the ruins of the Faith Answers, they would tend to be responsive, consultative, not just to the grand 'mass', the 'people', but also to its parts, the individuals. Without their Faith-Answer excuses, political movements could no longer cover up their arrogance, stupidity and cruelty with transcendent rationalizing. Officials would either have to change their attitudes or leave office. The power-interplay between the whole and the parts could no longer be perverted by the centre's capacity to reward and punish by defining good and evil.

If no man-made absolute can resist the effects of change then perhaps would-be worshippers should erect cult statues to the god 'Change'. But 'change' is a paradoxical constant – the antithesis of what a Faith Answer system needs. Change defeats but cannot make permanent. It may be felt metaphysically, even emotionally – a highly recommended 'trip'– but it can never be concretized. It is a great truth which like a geometric figure, is simply there – defying the possibility of any kind of institutionalization. So here is something of which man may be certain, a surpassing transcendent truth. But as the prospective worshippers rush for the good news, they should know that, like the anarchist Bakunin,[1] they cannot establish what is, in human application, a disestablishing force, unless of course, they disregard its essence.

And then they will only have deluded themselves. The

[1] Mikhail Bakunin (1814-1876), the guiding 'light' of 19th-century anarchism, planted political seeds that grew in Russia, Italy and, especially, Spain. Paradoxically, he governed his own organization, the Alliance of Socialist Democracy, like a despot while preaching the destruction of all organized power.

advantage of tolerating and accepting the paradoxical truth of change is metaphysically and practically positive. It reduces all forms of social organization to the status of totally amendable contracts. In the earthing of celestial certainties, man frees himself of their ritual demands upon his existence. He escapes the sense exactions of the Faith Answer and can now enlarge his own being by the unfettered expansion of sense perception in sound, taste, touch, aroma and vision.

In a social world where change is understood to be the only absolute, and where all action is tempered by the presence of paradox, much autonomy would return to the individual, and groups would have to justify themselves by responding to the membership, not only as to the construction of useful group goals, but the means of attaining them. A far more fluid balance would then exist between the needs of individuals and their contribution to groupings. With their perhaps once primordially-useful but now malignant 'super truth' excized, the catch-phrase 'power to the people' might become a reality. But not the version of Robespierre, Bakunin or Marx.

Instead, the pragmatic version – where the group's objective and means of attainment do not require the societal catharsis of gas chambers, deliberate starvation, firing squads, body and book burnings, and constant propagandizing, or the panoply of apparatus still developing in the field of mind control. How the future Robespierres would enjoy implementing their visions of the 'will of the people' through some supranational internet!

The 'beauties'– the poetry, pretty stories, ecstatic hopes – of the Faith Answer are siren songs of individual enslavement; they are the come-on, the barker's snake-oil pitch. That they can never be and never have been true is concealed by individual death and the current Faith Answer's self-serving revision of history. Newer and far more total devices of social oppression are becoming available which will make the control of past Faith Answers seem quite defective. And if the technology of man's mind and body control be combined with the technology of war in the service of more messianic Faith absolutes, the possibilities for human existence, let alone individual development, could be at an end.

Observing the historical collapse of all Faith Answers, their wasteful confrontation with change and their assault on individuals, should be a warning. Will the individual, seeing the danger to his subjective reality from 'objective truths', still allow his existence to be diminished in the building of more Faith pyramids? Alternatively can he face the paradox and the dynamic of existence and begin to explore and expand his subjective reality and perhaps his life at the expense of transcendent answers?

Who next?

#	Date	Event	Influence
1.	4 BC	Jesus is born	➜
2.	AD 30	High-point of his Ministry	➜
3.	30	Crucifixion	●
4.	60	Paul rescues Christianity	➜
5.	240	Christianity widespread	➜
6.	249-303	Decius and the Diocletian persecutions	●
7.	313	Constantine's Edict of Toleration	➜
8.	325	Council of Nicaea	➜
9.	361-3	Julian—Neo-paganism	●
10.	381	Theodosius establishes Christianity	➜
11.	413	Augustine's City of God	➜
12.	496	Clovis converted	➜
13.	604	Pope Gregory the 'Great'	➜
14.	655	Pope Martin dies under arrest	●
15.	678	Moslems fail to capture Constantinople	➜
16.	712	Moors capture Seville—Spain lost	●
17.	732	Charles Martell's victory at Tours against the Moors	➜
18.	772	Charlemagne confirms limited papal temporal power	➜
19.	846	Moslems take Sicily, Sardinia, Corsica, Balearic Islands	●
20.	864	False Decretals used to justify power	➜
21.	912	Conversion of the Normans	➜
22.	988	Conversion of the Russians	➜
23.	1046	Three rival popes—from this point reform begins	●
24.	1099	Capture of Jerusalem—the Crusades	➜
25.	1149	The Second Crusade is unsuccessful	●
26.	1187	Saladin reconquers Jerusalem	●
27.	1204	Capture of Constantinople by the Fourth Crusade	●
28.	1213	Albigensian Crusade against fellow Christians	●
29.	1233	Inquisition founded	➜
30.	1270	Death of St. Louis	➜
31.	1274	Death of Thomas Aquinas	➜
32.	1303	Pope imprisoned (Boniface VIII)	●
33.	1378	The Great Schism	●
34.	1384	Wycliffe, the reformer, dies	●
35.	1409	Year of the three popes	●
36.	1453	Turks capture Constantinople. Failure of the Council of Basel	●
37.	1492	Lorenzo de'Medici dies. Decretals proven false	●
38.	1521	Leo X bans Luther	➜
39.	1534	Henry VIII—Act of Supremacy	➜
40.	1543	Copernicus—Heliocentric Theory	➜
41.	1553	Calvin burns Servetus	➜
42.	1572	Tycho Brahe's Super Nova	➜
43.	1605	High-point of the Counter-reformation recovery	●
44.	1616	Copernicus placed on Index	●
45.	1624	Richelieu running France	●
46.	1632	Galileo forced to recant	●
47.	1687	Isaac Newton	●
48.	1721	Montesquieu's Lettres Persanes. (Clement XI dies)	●
49.	1740	Hume's Treatise on Human Nature. (Clement XII dies)	●
50.	1758	Diderot, Montesquieu, Voltaire. (Benedict XIV dies)	●
51.	1769	Diderot, Rousseau, d'Holbach. Decline of the Jesuits. (Clement XIII dies)	●
52.	1799	French Revolution, Gibbon. (Pius V dies)	➜
53.	1807	Hegel	➜
54.	1823	Post-French revolutionary recovery. (Pius VII dies)	➜
55.	1846	Alliance with reaction. Beagle's voyage. (Gregory XVI dies)	●
56.	1878	Darwin, Communist Manifesto, Papal Infallibility. (Pius IX dies)	●
57.	1903	Nietzsche, Das Kapital Vol 2, 3. (Leo XII dies)	●
58.	1914	Anti-modernist Pope Pius X dies	●
59.	1922	Einstein, Freud, Russian Revolution. (Benedict XV dies)	●
60.	1933	(-1939) Hitler, anti-clericalism in Mexico, Spain. (Pius XI dies)	●
61.	1958	Expansion of Marxism, Mao Tse-Tung. (Pius XII dies)	●
62.	1963	Vatican 11. John XXIII dies)	➜
63.	1978	Non-Catholic Revivalism. (Paul VI dies)	➜
64.	1983	Continuing Revivalism. (Papacy of John Paul II)	➜
65.	1990-5	Collapse of Marxism.	●

Appendix
CHART INTRODUCTION
AND CHART POINTS
(See Chart Points on page 174)

Introduction

Every Faith fails to bring about the earthly or heavenly effects it promises. But the latency of this realization, the degree of political control exercised by the Faith System and mass intellectual inertia combine to allow most failed Faiths to fade gradually rather than vanish overnight. Nor do they fade smoothly. Their 'sick-room' charts are full of spells of partial recovery followed by deep set-backs.

Catholic Christianity's chart shows a basic uptrend to the time of the Crusades,[1] and another with the appearance of Thomas Aquinas' *Summa Theologica*.[2] Then with the arrival of the 16th century, the 'secular' Popes, Alexander VI and Leo X, the split with Luther and scientific confrontation over the heliocentric and geocentric theories, it begins its definitive decline. The 'Enlightenment' and the Rousseauian French Revolution 'clobber' it, and just as it rallies in the l9th-century, it is hit by both Marxism and Darwinism.

The 20th-century experienced a tiny upswing as some saw Christianity as a countervailent to Dialectical Materialism; then came the crash of Vatican Two, the desanctifying of old-time saints, the revolt of the birth-controllers and the marrying priests, and the lack of bright young adepts. The arrival of Pope John Paul[3] changed nothing, yet his sincerity and old-time holiness and his insight into Marxism gave the Roman Catholic Faith Chart a small uptick.

A similar sick-room graph for Marxism would show a leap upward in 1848 with the publication of the Communist Manifesto and that year's revolutionary turmoil followed by sharp disappointment; then a high during the 1870-71 Paris Commune and again disillusionment after the Commune's destruction. 1907 would see a new high as the Tsar gave way on a number of points but then another drop after the autocracy re-established itself until Lenin's successful management of the post-Revolution sent the graph into its highest territory. There would be a moderate decline during the New Economic Policy and then a jag upwards but not to the old Lenin

---

[1] Chart points 24-28.
[2] Chartpoint 31.
[3] Chart point 64.

high when Stalin ended the very limited capitalism practiced during this policy. The signing of the Treaty of August 1939 with Hitler would show up as a violent fall, which would only be saved by the alliance with the West after the German invasion of Russia. Despite the Soviet military imposition of Marxist clergy at the helms of Eastern European governments, the graph would fall until it was suddenly jerked back up briefly by Mao's Marxism in the East and Castro's Marxism in the West; plus Marcuse's 'student-inspiring Marxism' of the late 60s. After the early 1970s the graph would have started to fall sharply. Underlined by Czechoslovakia's treatment of the dissidents, the 1981-82 union-busting efforts of the Polish Communist Party, the fatal Soviet military adventure in Afganistan. Then, of course, the Gorbachovian Glasnost-Peristroika debacle, which let light into a system that needed the dark to survive; followed by Gorbachov's fall, and the collapse of Communism itself. The chart would be bumping along the bottom only because China, at this writing, still calls itself Communist. Cuba has lost all 'street cred' and North Korea is only a fascist dictatorship dressed in Marxist hand-me-downs.

While the dates selected to illustrate this Christian Faith Chart are obviously arbitrary, the importance given to them via the vertical axis is even more so. There were more nominal Christians in the 20th-century than either in the year 1099 (Capture of Jerusalem – Chart 24) or 174 years later at the death of Thomas Aquinas (Chart 31), but the power of traditional Christian churches over them was greatly diminished. So the chart offers an imagined equation between the strength of Faith and the quantity of adherents.

The first event listed on the Chart occurs on the date given. Where other events are given, they fall within the era. After 1721 the Chart points are generally dated by the death of the reigning pope (shown in parenthesis).

The Appendix contains an explanation of the Chart points as well as other relevant information.

Points

1. 4-7 BC

Jesus is born. All the dates in Jesus Christ's life are uncertain. His birth was not later than 4 BC nor earlier than 7 BC. His period of ministry probably lasted not more than three years and began after he was thirty. An approximate date for the crucifixion might be 30 AD. The gospels were all written at least thirty to sixty years after Jesus' death, and they are hagiography rather than biography, so that the chronicle of his life lacks informative personal detail.

2. 30 AD

In the final year of his life and at the height of his personal power, Christ and his apostles create a stir in Palestine. Nobody really likes an occupying power even if it does bring law, order and bread. The Jewish religious officials were 'collaborators' with the Roman occupying forces, so when Jesus attacked the sterility and legalisms of the Sadducees and Pharisees it was an automatic crowd-pleaser. Such attacks also, despite Jesus' careful handling of them ('Render unto Caesar the things that are Caesar's...'), implied a policy of 'Romans go home'. He 'performed' the same obligatory miracles his contemporary competition performed and was apparently not especially avant garde in his ethical philosophy. What he did do, which probably set him apart, was that he presented himself as a continuer, although radical updater, of the old and proven Jewish religion. These elements, combined with what must have been an astonishing personal charisma, gave the movement a strong initial impetus.

3. 30/36 AD

Christ is executed, circa 30/36 AD. At this point, deprived of its principal impetus, Christianity was probably headed toward oblivion.

4. 60 AD

50 to 60 AD, Paul rescued Christianity, adding some 'Christocentric' features and clarifying (within the mystical frame) certain doctrinal elements, as well as probably inventing some new ones. His building of a network of geographically separated letter-writing Christian

adepts (slightly reminiscent of the American pre-revolutionary com-
mittees of correspondence) went a long way toward unifying both
movement and doctrine. His setting free Christianity from Jewish
observance opened the way for the 'church universal', as well as disassociating it from the Jewish debacle of 70 AD (the capture of
Jerusalem by Titus).

5. 240 AD

The Christian cult over the years proselytized successfully throughout a great part of the Roman empire, constructed (or reconstructed)
the four gospels – Matthew, Mark, Luke and John – and was becoming a political factor to be reckoned with.

6. 249 and 303 AD

The first broad institutional attempt to suppress Christianity by the
Emperor Decius (249 AD) was short-lived as he was killed in battle
in 251 AD. The second, by Diocletian in 303 AD, was more serious,
since it involved execution of cult leaders, loss of civil rights, and lia-
bility, regardless of class, to torture. Subsequent decrees before his
retirement included the death penalty for 'unrecanting' Christians.
   During this period and up to about 308 AD, when Diocletian
briefly came out of retirement, Christianity's closest competition, the
cult of Mithra, looked like a possible winner. It was widespread, particularly in the army, but its basically polytheistic base, when
monotheism was 'in', its exclusion of women, and its mythical rather
than flesh-and-blood saviour figure fatally damaged its capacity to
compete successfully with Christianity.

7. 313 AD

Circa 313 AD in Milan, the Emperor Constantine, as prime mover,
issued what amounted to an edict officially tolerating Christian religious practice.

8. 325 AD

The Council of Nicaea was convoked in 325 AD by Constantine, who,
having eliminated his last rival, was able to involve himself, alias the
State, in doctrinal matters. This Council, convened not far from the

Emperor's summer palace in Nicomedia, was designed to solidify dogma, especially concerning the nature of Jesus. Arius, a presbyter in Alexandria, was pushing the divisive idea that Jesus as a creation of god was not of one substance with God. The Council decided against him. The sharp rise in the graph is because the Church-State amalgam was by now virtually established.

9. 361-363 AD

Julian 361-363 AD, was called the 'apostate' by the Christians, because of his attempt to restore paganism – or rather his personal view of how paganism should have been. This point also coincides with the last hopes of Mithraism, since Julian was also a Mithra convert. But for his death, the decline of Christianity might have been greater; however, the basically tolerant paganism of the time could never have succeeded long against the increasingly elaborated and exclusivist intolerance of highly organized Christianity.

10. 381 AD

Theodosius 'the Great' made paganism a crime in 380-381 AD, establishing Christianity as the exclusive State-Religion. At this time St. Jerome began work on the vulgate Latin translation of the Bible.

11. 413 AD

Beginning in 413 AD, three years after Alaric's sack of Rome, Augustine began writing his City of God – 'the City of God endureth forever though the greatest City on earth has fallen.' Theologians, by picking here and there in his writings, fortified Christianity's intellectual-mystical foundations.

12. 496 AD

Despite disastrous political conditions in the Western Roman Empire, the continuing barbarian incursions, the pillaging and general collapse of lay authority, the Christianization of the Gothic invaders and the strength of the papacy increased. Clovis, the king of the Franks, was converted around 496 AD.

13. 604 AD

In 589 AD, through King Reccared's conversion, Visigothic Spain became Christian. Between 590-604 AD, Pope Gregory 'the Great' laid the ground for papal absolutism, and in 596 AD sent Augustine of Canterbury on a mission which successfully converted England to Christianity.

14. 655 AD

In 649 AD the Eastern Emperor's religious stance was attacked by the Lateran (Roman) Synod. In 653 AD the Exarch (Eastern Emperor's executive representative) had Pope Martin I arrested and sent to the East, where he died in 655 AD. The importance of these events – squabbling over the nature of Christ – is that the Eastern and Western churches were moving toward a basically permanent de facto, if not *de jure*, schism.

15. 678 AD

After conquering all Syria, Egypt, North Africa to the eastern extreme of Algeria, the Moslem blockade of Constantinople (673-678 AD) failed. The Moslems were assisted in taking over Christian areas by the doctrinal differences between those churches and Constantinople.

16. 712 AD

In 712 AD, the 'Moors' captured Seville and the rest of the Iberian peninsula fell rapidly as the armies advanced. Although the Moslems were far more tolerant than the Christians, there were still a great many Christians who abjured and accepted Islam. The Jews welcomed the invaders as liberators because of their sufferings under Christianity.

17. 732 AD

In 732 AD, but for Charles Martell's victory at Tours (Poitiers), the Moslem religion and political power might have over-run much or even all of Europe.

18. 772 AD

Charlemagne defeated the Lombards, who were menacing papal temporal power, and in 772 AD confirmed the 'donation of Pepin' (756 AD), which gave the papacy the right (at any rate the usufruct) to found papal states in Italy. This is, perhaps, a deceptive upward move on the chart because it was in pursuit of this temporal phantasmagoria that the 15th-16th century papacy was to produce Savonarola, Cesare Borgia and Martin Luther – an undignified and almost catastrophic moment for Roman Catholicism.

19. 846 AD

The scope of Christianity in the Mediterranean was reduced considerably by the Moslem invasion of Sicily, Sardinia, Corsica and the Balearic Islands (827-831 AD). The year 846 AD, when Sergius, the Duke of Naples, defeated the Moslems in a sea battle, seems to mark their limit of expansion.

20. 864 AD

The mid-9th century saw more East-West church in-fighting with the one important pope – Nicholas I (858-867 AD) – continuing the centralizing of papal power, especially the right of appeal to Rome. If he did not know that the 'Decretals' he cited in 865 AD were forged, he would have been more naive than he seems to have been. These documents probably first appeared in Rome in 864 AD and were as useful for the justifying of the Pope's supremacy as if they had been tailored to papal specifications.

21. 912 AD

The conversion of Rollo (Christianized Robert) of Normandy took place in 912 AD. After Pope Nicolas I's death and the increasing decentralization of Western political power, the papacy also declined. In the first quarter of the 10th century the Norsemen consolidated the results of their invasions of Europe. Despite the weakened state of the papacy, Christianity itself was so well-rooted, so well-supplied with 'answers' that the invaders were converted. (They brought with them a very weakly adumbrated mythology, which even Reichsfuehrer SS Heinrich Himmler failed to connect up logically). In the East the Orthodox Church had managed to deal, at least partially with the invading Bulgars by converting them in 870 AD.

22. 988 AD

The conversion of Vladimir, Grand Duke of Kiev, in 988 AD, resulted in the Russians joining the Greek Orthodox Church. It is said that he sent envoys to 'shop' for the most attractive religion, Western or Eastern Christianity or Mohammedanism. They were most impressed by the orthodox ritual. Even though he had many wives, at least one taken by force after killing her father, he was immediately turned into a saint by the Church.

23. 1046 AD

1046 AD was a year of three rival popes – Gregory Vl, Sylvester II and Benedict IX. All three were deposed in the synods of Sutri and Rome under pressure by the Emperor Henry III. After this the Papacy began a reform – prohibitions against simony and marriage, leading towards the most powerful period of both the Papacy and Western Christianity. In 1054, the last year of the reforming Pope Leo IX (1049-1054), the de facto schism between the Eastern and Western churches was officially recognized. During the Crusades, and subsequently, diplomats, dogmatists, and warriors have tried to put that 'Humpty-Dumpty' back together without real success.

24. 1099 AD

Beginning in 1073 AD with Pope Gregory VII and ending with the realisation of the Crusader's dream, the conquest of Jerusalem in 1099, the last quarter of the 11th-century shows a sharp move upwards in the Chart. Gregory VII, having studied those forged Decretals (but in his case not being much of a scholar and perhaps not realizing they were forged), went further than any other Pope in claims of power: 1. The Church never erred nor could err. 2. The Pope could depose an Emperor, depose or reimpose Bishops; only he could call synods, and he was the supreme Judge without appeal. (Imagine how quickly these claims would be diagnosed as paranoia if the claimant did not have a huge organization behind him.) The incredible success of the first crusade crowned the papacy's efforts at reform. Meanwhile in Spain, Alfonso VI of Castile took a significant step in the Christian reconquest by capturing Toledo (1085 AD). Sicily was 'liberated' from Moslem rule by the Normans, now Christianized (1072-1091 AD).

25. 1149 AD

The second crusade (1147-1149 AD) failed to achieve anything of importance except to sour relations with the Eastern Empire by plundering the Balkans. The crusading movement was damaged.

26. 1187 AD

Jerusalem was taken by Saladin, reducing the crusaders' conquests to small enclaves. The second crusade was preached by a reportedly reluctant Bernard of Clairvaux and sponsored by Pope Eugenius III, but the third crusade (1189-1192 AD) was entirely controlled by non-ecclesiastical powers – Richard I, 'the Lion Heart' and Philip II of France. It obtained a very modest success, and with Richard ordering the slaughtering of 3,000 prisoners because the first instalment of the agreed ransom was delayed, could hardly be considered a net gain for Christian ethics.

27. 1204 AD

The cynical hypocrisy of the fourth crusade (1203-1204), in which Christian Constantinople was taken, plundered and raped by brother Christians, may only find its parallel in the 'cover-up' Marxist rhetoric employed to justify the Hitler-Stalin pact of August 1939 – the pact that made war feasible for Hitler and profitable for Stalin.

28. 1213 AD

The Albigensian (Waldensian) Crusade preached by Innocent III against fellow but slightly differing Christians practically obliterated the advanced culture of Provence. Simon de Montfort captured Maret in 1213 after the Pope, too late, tried to send the crusaders against the Moslems of Spain. (This period was a great time for cathedral building – Chartres c. 1194, Amiens c. 1200, Rheims, c. 1210.)

29. 1233 AD

Pope Gregory IX in 1233 gave the Dominican order the job of investigating heresy and required the Bishops to cooperate. St. Louis approved what was the juridical establishment of a permanent inquisition. The chart does not treat this event as a weakness; after all, the strength of a Faith Answer is the degree to which it can enforce its paranoic logic. Intolerance is also a measure of organized faith.

30. 1270 AD

Louis IX of France, later St. Louis (1226-1270), did much personally to restore respect for the Church, as well as, by his own example, act as a mirror of Christian principles. He participated in the seventh and eighth crusades, both failures, dying on the way home in Tunis, where he hoped to convert the Sultan. During Louis's reign Cordoba, in 1236, and Seville in 1248 AD, are added to Christian Spain.

31. 1274 AD

At the death of Thomas Aquinas (1274), the intellectual synthesis of Christianity, classical learning, reason and religion reached perhaps its highest point in his *Summa Theologica*.

32. 1303 AD

The intellectual triumph of Aquinas was not matched by the papacy, which, broadly speaking, experienced an extended decline. Boniface VIII claimed, through the *Bull Unum Sanctum*, superiority over all lay authority. A year later (1303) he was taken prisoner by Nogaret and Colonna: He was to be taken to France on orders of Philip IV to be tried, but died in the same year. Two years later the papacy moved to Avignon, remaining there from 1305-1378. Nation states were no longer willing to accept papal superiority.

33. 1378 AD

In 1378 the 'Great Schism' began, during which there were rival popes in Avignon and Rome. Organized Western Christianity went into a stage of vertiginous descent.

34. 1384 AD

John Wycliffe (1320-1384), English church-reformer, even denied the doctrine of transubstantiation in 1381 in *De Eucharista* and got away with it, at least in his lifetime, although, as an absurd aside, his remains were dug up and burned in 1428 by order of Pope Martin V pursuant to the 4 May 1415 decision of the Council of Constance.

35. 1409 AD

In 1409, while Giovanni de' Medici was making a great banking fortune, the Council of Pisa tried to put an end to the 'Great Schism' by electing a new Pope, Alexander V. But, because the rival Popes Gregory XII and Benedict XIII refused to resign, there were now three Popes instead of two. It is not at all difficult to imagine what this Marx Brothers situation did for Western institutionalized Christianity. Neither is it surprising that a Church reformer should appear five years later at the reform-oriented Council of Constance and say that sin destroys the value of clerical office nor that he, John Hus, should be executed in 1415 by that 'reforming' council in flagrant violation of the immunity he had been promised!

36. 1453 AD

In 1453 Constantinople's capture by the Turks had very little significance for Christianity. The Greek Orthodox Church had remained, as its name suggests, just that, unchanged and unchanging for several centuries. The time was long past when it was a centre or source of controversy. Politically, of course, the final collapse of the Eastern Empire (well prepared by the invaders of the fourth crusade) was very significant, since it opened wide the Balkans to the Ottoman Turks. More important for its subsequent effects on the Christian Church was the dissolution of the Council of Basel (1431-1449) in 1449 without even enacting moderate reforms.

37. 1492 AD

Lorenzo de' Medici died in 1492, as did Pope Innocent VIII. The popes, like the whole intellectual and social 'upper crust' of Italy, were taken up with the 'delights' of the Renaissance, which were primarily secular, even pagan. Nicholas V, who had been librarian to

Cosimo de' Medici, brought the Humanist movement to the Vatican. Among his litterateurs was none other than Lorenzo Valla, who proved that the 'Decretals', used for centuries by Popes to provide a juridical basis for their power, were fake. Pius II (1458-1464) was another humanist and himself an accomplished writer. Sixtus IV (1471-1484), a party to an assassination conspiracy (Pazzi), also built the Sistine Chapel (1473), patronized Botticelli, Pintoricchio and many other artists. Innocent VIII (1484-1492) even went so far as to recognize his children. In that same year (1492) another reformer, Girolamo Savonarola, imagined himself the sword of the Lord (Gladius Domini) and tried to reform Florence, ending up on a bon-fire on 23 May 1498. It is said that Pope Alexander VI (1492-1503), ordering Savonarola's death, said: 'Even though he were a second John the Baptist... 'His children, his outrageous politique, the con-dottieri activities of his son Cesare Borgia, the disgraceful (in a Christian sense) political marriages and annulments of his daughter Lucrezia, probably bring the papacy to a Christian, although not a political, low. However, the almost anti-Christian challenge of the Renaissance never penetrated very deeply, and it was the Establishment that got the blame, not the ideas, and reform was con-fidently expected to 'fix things up'.

38. 1521 AD

Leo X's (Giovanni de' Medici 1513-1521) principal reaction to the reformer Martin Luther (1483-1546) was to ban him in 1521. Under the previous Pope, Julius II (1503-1513) some reforms had been begun, but now the Reformation had started, and only the most rad-ical changes would have had any effect. The chart-line after this low point rises because despite the discomfiture of the papacy, Christianity, through the Reformation, began to make intellectual and spiritual headway against the fashions of the Renaissance.

39. 1534 AD

The enactment in 1534 of the Act of Supremacy, substituting the Crown of England for the Pope of Rome, is again more of a shock to the papacy than to Christianity. Even the 1536-1539 suppression of the monasteries seems not to have shaken the Faith. These events can be fitted into the general context of the Reformation even if they were triggered by Henry VIII's (1491-1547) marriage and fiscal policies. In these years the Spanish conquistadors were in the process of subduing Mexico, Peru and Venezuela (inter alia), adding gold to the royal treasury and millions of Christian converts to the Catholic Church.

40. 1543 AD

Nicolaus Copernicus' (1473-1543) publication of *De Revolutionibus Orbium Coelestium* in the last year of his life had no instant effect on either astronomy or the doctrines of the church. Probably to diminish the risks in publishing it, a note was added without Copernicus' knowledge saying that the heliocentric theory was just an easy way of computing planetary movements! It was read only by the learned, and lay about like a time bomb amongst the doctrinal rigidities of the Church.

41. 1553 AD

With the Reformation 'raging', Calvin (1509-1564), lately the pleader for tolerance, executed Servetus in Geneva (1553) for denying the Trinity. Meanwhile Anne du Bourg, a prominent member of the Paris parlement, was executed in 1559 through the offices of the Catholic Church for merely objecting to persecution. In 1562 some Protestants were celebrating a church service in a barn in Vassy. The Duke de Guise sent his men-at-arms to turn them out. When they refused to leave, 68 were killed. These sad events are unfortunately a symptom of the revival of Western Christianity. Tolerance is not a characteristic of organized Faith. In 1545 three thousand Waldensians, now affiliated with Lutheranism, from hill towns in Southern France whose families had for many years escaped the Catholic searchers, were slaughtered. The martyr statistics of the 16th century are an important element in the rising graph line.

42. 1572 AD

Tycho Brahe (1546-1601) in 1572 observed a super nova, thereby destroying the Church-supported Aristotelian idea that the heavens never changed. But this assault on changelessness had no effect on the Counter-Reformation papacy which was in high gear with, for a change, a series of hardworking, clean-living Popes, one of whom, Pius V (1556-1572), was canonized in 1712. During this period the catechism (1556), new breviary (1568), and missal (1570) were published, incorporating decisions of the Council of Trent (1547-1549). The reforming effects of the 1540 founding of the Society of Jesus (the Jesuits) began to be felt throughout Catholic Christendom.

43. 1605 AD

The year 1605 marks the peak of the recovery of the Catholic Church. From now on the papacy, under Paul V (1605-1621), sinks back into some of its nepotistic luxuriant habits. The interdict against Venice (1606) failed. It was to be the last time this device was used against a sovereign entity.

44. 1616 AD

While Pope Paul V was arranging the Borghese family fortunes, Copernicus' *De Revolutionibus* was placed on the index of prohibited books (1616). Although heliocentricity as a theory had never been acceptable to the Christian Church, there was now beginning that open, brittle and, in the end, deeply damaging struggle between Christian theology and science. In 1609 Johannes Kepler (1571-1630) set out laws for elliptical planetary orbits and gave astronomy its name.

45. 1624 AD

From 1624-1642, a Cardinal was running France, ruthlessly scheming and plotting to concentrate supreme political power in the Crown. Richelieu's manoeuvres were, from a Machiavellian viewpoint, brilliant, but they were no advertisement for 'reformed' Roman Catholicism.

46. 1632 AD

Galileo Galilei (1564-1642), using the newly-invented telescope, compiled results that demolished the church-supported geocentric theories of Aristotle and Ptolemy. He wrote a dialogue *(1632)* between earth-centred and sun-centred theories in which the latter was obviously superior. As a result he was forced to recant by the Inquisition. Rene Descartes (1596-1650) was on the point of publishing *Le Monde,* which would have affirmed the Copernican theory, but just in time heard about Galileo's difficulties with the Inquisition. He stopped its

publication. Several years later, and after he had altered its cos-
mogony to get by the Inquisition, he published his great *Discours de
la Méthode* (1637).

47. 1687 AD

The rest of the 17th-century saw a body of science appearing that,
apart from the increasingly distant credits to God, really did nothing
to confirm theology. In *1687* Isaac Newton's (1642-1727) *Philosophiae
Naturalis Principia Mathematica* contained his three laws of motion,
the first of which states that bodies once set in motion will continue
that motion until impeded by an external cause. If indeed God had
started it (as Newton thought), he was not needed to keep it going.

From 1655 a series of non-nepotistic honest Popes did what they
could, which was very little, to hold back the high tide of secularism.
Innocent XI (1676-1689) was, on balance, defeated by Louis XIV in the
strengthening of royal power over papal power. Louis XIV later, in
1697, retracted his gains, evidently to keep the papacy with him over
his plans for the Spanish succession. The same class of dispute continued throughout the 18th century, culminating in the invasion of
the papal lands by French armies (1796) and removal of Pope Pius VI
to France, where he died.

The 17th-century forces arrayed, without intention or collusion,
against Christian dogma were formidable. Each increment in scientific knowledge seemed further to displace the strength of Christian
assertions. None of the great scientists were atheists, nor were the
philosophers, although each one was generally responsible for nar-
rowing or altering the medieval conceptions of God. Even so 'God-
centred' a philosopher as Spinoza (1632-1677) was unwelcome to
both Jews and Christians. Hobbes (1588-1679) lets God be a first
mover and denies 'transubstantiation'. Rene Descartes (1596-1650)
produced a deterministic material world where there seems to be no
logical need for the soul, although he put it in and gave it the power
to change the direction of the motion of 'vital spirits'! Leibnitz (1646-
1716) was so upset by the discrepancies arising from his studies in
mathematical logic and Aristotle's doctrine of the syllogism that he
never published the results of his work. Man had to wait another 150
years before mathematical logic was again invented, all because of
Leibnitz' respect for Aristotle and, one suspects, his connection to the
Christian dogma still defended by the Church. Despite John Locke's
(1632-1704) strong Christian beliefs, he founded 'empiricism' and

wrote that 'revelation must be judged by reason'.

The 17th-century chart-line is continually descending as Christian assertions are unwillingly, even unconsciously, attacked by both science and philosophy.

Usually, after prolonged periods of decline in 'market' charts, there is some mild recovery, perhaps followed by a further decline. But, in the 18th century, it is impossible to find much or even any significant recovery of Christianity in general, and, specifically, none in the papacy. 18th-century Protestantism was also increasingly permeated by the rationalism and scientific approach of the Enlightenment. In fact, it was usually to Protestant countries, Switzerland, England and Holland in particular, that persecuted 'new wave' intellectuals fled. As such figures as Jean Jacques Rousseau, and especially Voltaire, became *a la mode,* they found it easier to find protection, even in Catholic countries.

It was the non-churchmen, scientists, philosophers and ethico-political proposers who were the prime movers of the century. Charles Louis de Secondat, Baron de Montesquieu (1689-1755), Voltaire (1694-1778), David Hume (1711-1776), Jean Jacques Rousseau (1712-1778), Denis Diderot (1713-1784), Immanuel Kant (1724-1804), among many others, wielded far greater influence than any Pope or Protestant theologian. The scientists and their discoveries never added anything to buttress Christian theory – Protestant or Catholic. Their work, when combined, served to support the anti-dogmatic and anti-clerical argumentation of the Enlightenment:

48. 1721 AD

At the death of Clement XI (1700-1721) the papacy had been seriously damaged by its efforts to intervene in the War of the Spanish Succession. Its peacemaking efforts actually did it harm. Efforts via the *Bull Unigenitus* to deal with the Jansenists were a failure, and the one bright spot, missionary activity, was similarly disastrously bungled. The publication in the same year as Clement's death of Montesquieu's (1689-1755) *Lettres Persanes* (European society as seen through Persian eyes) is of more significance for the tone of the 18th-century than the Pope's demise.

49. 1740 AD

Pope Clement XII dies. He succeeded Benedict XIII, whose confidant, Cardinal Coscia, had helped himself to the papal till to such an extent that the papacy was in serious financial straits. Clement was gout-ridden and 78 and ignored in European political settlements. In 1739-1740 David Hume's (1711-1776) *Treatise on Human Nature* was published. This was the work Kant (1724-1804) said awakened him from his 'dogmatic slumbers'. Hume considered that no belief was based on reason.

50. 1758 AD

Benedict XIV (1740-1758) was more than a cut above the previous popes intellectually, but was it appropriate for him to be corresponding amicably with Voltaire, the uncrowned leader of the anti-Christian movement, as well as sending him two gold medals? This Pope must also bear the responsibility for the ruination of the promising missionary movements in China and Malabar. During this papacy Denis Diderot's (1713-1784) *Lettres sur les Aveugles* (blind) and *Lettres sur les Sourds et Muets* (Deaf and Dumb) were published (1749 and 1751 respectively), advancing to some extent the principle of relativity and in one case applying it to God, the last essay prefiguring Darwinism in its suggestion that variation and better adaptability may be associated with biological survival. This cost him three months in Vincennes prison. In 1748 Montesquieu's enormously important political tract *L'Ésprit des Lois* (Spirit of Laws) was published.

51. 1769 AD

1758-1769 were intellectually and religiously disastrous years for Christian dogmatics. Clement XIII (1758-1769) was forced to abandon the Jesuit order, the hardest-working proselytizers for the papacy. The actual winding-up of the order came under the next Pope, since Clement died of a stroke when the Catholic nations' ambassadors demanded total dissolution. The intellectual and, via Rousseau (1712-1778), emotional tide of the enlightenment was at flood. Although Diderot's *Encyclopaedia* was banned in 1759, he was still able to finish it by 1765. It did not propose atheism or tear down the Church's mysteries. But with all its scientific solutions to earth problems God was left with very little to do. Rousseau's *Julie: Ou La Novelle Héloise* (1761) and the *Contrat Social* (1762) are not anti-Christian, but anti-establishment; Genevan Protestantism consigned them to the bonfire. In 1761 a genuinely atheistic book appeared, *Le Christianisme Dévoilé*, written by Diderot's friend and host, Baron d'Holbach (1723-1789).

Christianity is seen to be at the bottom of the world's evils, *a priori* arguments for the deity's existence are rejected, the thing men label as 'soul' dies with the body, and if vice renders man happy, 'He should love vice.'

52. 1799 AD

Pope Clement XIV (1769-1774) finished off the Jesuits to 'avoid schism' (1773) and Pope Pius VI (1775-1799), hopelessly ostentatious and irresponsible, died a prisoner of the French armies – hardly the adequate papal response to the challenge of the French Revolution! Edward Gibbon (1737-1794) completed his last volume of *The History of the Decline and Fall of the Roman Empire* (1788), driving still another nail into the intellectual coffin of Christianity by assigning the latter an impressive share in the destruction of the Roman Empire. But there were other nails being driven for a change into a new coffin – that of the Enlightenment by the ghastly excesses of the French Revolution (1789-94). Christianity and the papacy survived, but the Enlightenment didn't. Those very excesses were what made the Catholic-Christian revival of the early 19th-century possible. Marie-Jean Condorcet's (1743-1794) death on the guillotine can stand for the many scientists, scholars and thinkers 'lopped' off, sometimes literally, by the Revolution. His *Tableau Historique des Progrés de l'Ésprit Humain,* dealing optimistically with human perfectability and demonstrating man's progress, was published posthumously in 1795.

The 19th-century saw Christianity retreating from the concrete toward the spiritual. Such a retreat was begun early, especially in Protestant circles.

53. 1807 AD

Georg W F Hegel (1770-1831) provided the 19th-century with an intellectualized base for Protestantism, Marxism and academic philosophy. In addition, if any State needed a philosopher to buttress its whims, Hegel would be that philosopher. His *Phanomenologie des Geistes (Phenomenology of the Mind)* was published in 1807.

54. 1823 AD

Pope Pius VII (1800-1823) recognized in the 1801 Concordat the material part of the French Revolution – loss of papal territory, the loss of Church properties, but obtained a State-supported hierarchy, and the declaration that France was a Catholic country. The relationship with Napoleon rapidly soured, until in 1808-1809 French troops entered the Papal States. Pius excommunicated the Emperor he had crowned just five years earlier and Napoleon had him arrested and taken off to France. Since the rest of Europe had become, or was becoming, disenchanted politically with the Emperor, the Pope as a martyr looked better every year. In the post-Napoleonic settlements the papacy received back its territory (except the French part), improved Church-State concordats, restored the Jesuit order, and became allied with the forces of European 'stability' personified in Austria's Prince Metternich. This alliance, initially valuable for the restored papacy, was to become a millstone later as the forces of Italian nationalism were attacked by papal allies. The chart line moves up sharply, not only for the revivified papacy, but for the vigorous activities of the German Protestants. In 1821-1822 Friedrich Schleiermacher (1768-1834) published his rejection of dogmatism, setting individual emotions free to find a more personal God. His *Der Christliche Glaube (Christian Faith)* was widely read in theological circles and his lectures were influential in the Protestant world. Relatively unimportant for its influence at the time of its publication (1819), Arthur Schopenhauer's (1788-1860) *Die Welt als Wille und Vorstellung (The World as Will and Idea)* was a time bomb of pessimism, to explode along with Nietzschean anti-Christianity late in the century.

55. 1846 AD

Gregory XVI (1831-1846), under pressure, removed the ultramontane Archbishop of Cologne in 1837, a year after Darwin (1808-1882) returned from his six-year voyage of *The Beagle*. The Pope condemned rational naturalism in an encyclical dated August 15, 1832. He opposed the separation of Church and State, liberty of conscience and the free press. The Church of Rome was battling all the intellectual, social and even religious trends of its time. As an age-old colossus, it could not do a *volte-face* the way some of the Protestants could. The intellectual and emotional *avant garde* of Christianity was beyond papal comprehension or control. In 1835 David Friedrich Strauss'

Leben Jesu (Life of Jesus) and later in 1840-1841 *Der Christliche Glaubenslehre... (Readings on the Christian Faith)* caused a sensation, the latter showing that the history of doctrines is their disintegration. Between 1843-1845 Soren Kierkegaard (1813-1855) published several important writings, of which *Euten-Eller (Either-Or)* is the best known. He maintained that in choosing Christ or the world it is useless to look for logical reasons – existential Christianity. It is up to the individual whether or not he takes the 'leap of faith'. All these trends such as the drive for the political unification of Italy, the anti-hierarchical 'illogicality' of revealed Faith, and the steadily mounting scientific discoveries which never confirmed dogma, were forces that the papacy seemed only to reject in a Canute-like manner, anathematizing the tide. The graph line moves higher up to Gregory's death partly because of Christian 'intellectual' ferment in the Protestant North.

56. 1878 AD

The long pontificate of Pius IX (1846-1878) comprehends some of the most important moments of the 19th-century. The 1848 *Communist Manifesto,* Charles Darwin's (1809-1882) *Origin of the Species by Means of Natural Selection* in 1859, the foundation by Karl Marx (1818-1883) of the 'First International Workingmen's Association' in 1864, the publication in 1867 of the first volume of *Das Kapital,* the completion of the unification of Italy with the annexation of Rome in 1870, were all in one way or another discomforting even for the 'liberal' that Pope Pius seemed to want to be. The beginnings of 'practical' communism, which proclaimed an active atheism, added to Darwin's 'unbiblical' creation story, were the two heaviest blows to fall on orthodox Christianity in the 19th century. The loss of the papal states and the failure of the papacy to take a positive position in the unification of Italy are uncompensated by the final papal pretension – infallibility (Vatican Council 1870). This was, to some extent, within the context of basic decline, a positive period of concentration of papal control of regional jurisdictions and restoration of the hierarchy in the Netherlands and Germany (1853). Politically Pius IX relied excessively on the French to maintain his temporal power. He, himself, built a band of devoted ecclesiastical supporters. As an addendum to this much beset papacy and the rise of 'scientific' Marxism comes Mary Baker Eddy's book (1875) *Science and Health...,* signalling the establishment of yet another science – Christian Science.

57. 1903 AD

The pontificate of Leo XIII (1878-1903) is involved in a decline in the general position of Christianity despite the Pope's impressive efforts to come to terms with science, the working-class question (1891), his efforts at oecumenism (the Greek Orthodox and English Protestant churches), his work with the missions, his ability to settle disputes (Switzerland and South American republics) and a broadened interpretation of the Bible in view of present day knowledge.

In 1885 and 1894 the final volumes of *Das Kapital* were published. Friederich von Nietzsche's *Der Antichrist* (1895) *(The Anti-Christ),* as the title suggests, is absolutely anti-Christian. The *New Testament* is the gospel of a completely ignoble species of man. A number of his concepts were 'usefully' removed from context in the formation of the muddled Nazi Faith Answer.

The explosion of science, theoretical and applied, continued – automobiles, telephones, electric light, motion pictures – and in the year of Pope Leo's death (1903), Orville Wright (1871-1948) and Wilbur Wright (1867-1912) flew the first successful heavier-than-air plane. Where did the papacy fit in? Who would say of 1903 'Oh yes, the year the good Pope Leo died' instead of 'The dawn of aviation – the Wright brothers'?

The 20th-century generally continues the Christian downtrend, with Marxism and, on a much smaller worldwide scale, Nazism, drawing off enthusiastic converts which in another age Christianity might have monopolized. The major persecutions of Christians after the Russian Revolution, and to a lesser degree under the Nazis, did not lead to any significant revival, except as a repository of protest. Marriages, abortions, divorces, birth-prevention, education, *et al* are freed or are being freed of Church control. Recruiting efforts to obtain replacement priests are not very fruitful, but 20th-century terrorist organizations have had to turn adepts away. It is the high emotion, low intellectual-content sects of Christianity that numerically 'hold their own'. Their crop of converts comes from a human yearning for ecstasy at the expense of empiricism (and a present fashion for rejecting scientific procedures).

58. 1914 AD

Pius X (1903-1914, canonized 1954) was still trying to put 'Humpty Dumpty' back together again. As a result, saint though he may have been, his policy was conservative to the point of being reactionary.

59. 1922 AD

While Benedict XV (1914-1922) (good diplomat though he was) failed to bring about a European peace, Albert Einstein (1879-1955) in 1914 published his *General Theory of Relativity.* The creation story now moves definitively to the region of literary myth. The Einsteinian world does not allow for the way God permitted himself to ignore the rules of the space-time continuum. In addition, the theological implications of relativity are destructive to man-made absolutes, since that which is observed depends on the observer and his point of reference. Another kind of subjectivity was beginning to be accepted through the writings of Sigmund Freud (1856-1939), where God was only involved if God formed a part of the patient's pathological picture.

In the confessional, absolution was obtained merely by reciting infractions against the laws of an objective absolute. This might or might not relieve the tensions of the 'sinner'. In psychoanalysis the patient's recital of personal detail is in search of explaining and curing a neurosis. The patient himself is at the centre – God is completely unnecessary.

The atheistic Russian Revolution in 1917 is part of the sharp decline that Christianity as a whole experienced during this papacy. Atheism had been rising for years, but with the political enshrinement of Marxism in Russia and the hyperactive imagination of Western artist-intellectuals of the twenties and thirties, fantasizing the charms of Russian socialism, 'godlessness' began to be *a la mode.*

60. 1939 AD

Pope Pius Xl (1922-1939) protested against the anti-clericalism in Mexico in 1926, and in 1931 the creeping revolution in the most Catholic of countries, Spain, brought church burnings, murders of priests, monks and nuns. The Pope tried to make his position clear by criticizing the maldistribution of wealth, while at the same time descrying the excesses of the revolutionists. He still condemned both socialism and communism. At least there was some small success in the Lateran Treaty (1929) and concordat with the Fascist government of Italy defining the Church's position and powers. The Pope now had temporal power in the few acres of Vatican City. A concordat was also signed with the Nazis without really improving matters. The assault on German Christianity via atheism and neo-paganism continued. The Church was, in the Thirties, faced with two antagonistic Faith Answers, the Nazi and the Marxist. The enemies were no longer obscure heretics, schisms or disobedient sovereigns. These, in comparison, were past luxuries. The attack now was on Christianity itself.

61. 1958 AD

Pope Pius XII (1939-1958) lived through some of the most difficult years the papacy has experienced. Trapped almost at the centre of the Second World War, Pius has been accused of not speaking out sufficiently forcefully against Hitler's racial policies (if extermination may be crowned with such an epithet). The enormity of the 'final solution' was not even accepted by the Jews themselves until the latter part of the war. It was not even believed by Allied Intelligence until millions had died. The Vatican in 1943-1944 was a precarious enclave in German-occupied Rome, teeming with 'illegal' refugees, many of whom were Jews. 'Speaking out' would have doomed these people and destroyed the usefulness – even the existence – of the Vatican. Hitler repeatedly expressed his desire to invade the Vatican and punish the Pope. By the summer of 1944 when the extermination of the Hungarian Jews had begun, the allies still could not be persuaded to bomb the railway line from Budapest to Poland.

The proclamation of the People's Republic of China on 1 October 1949, and the subsequent dismantling of all missionary activity ended hopes for the Christianizing of a major part of the world's population. The Marxist Faith Answer was clearly in ascendancy. In 1949 a Vatican decree of excommunication was launched against those Catholics who freely and consciously supported communism. The canonization of Pope Pius X took place in 1964. The U.S. exploded a hydrogen bomb two months earlier.

62. 1963 AD

Pope John XXIII (1958-1963) called for more voice for workers in industry (1961) and condemned materialism. In 1962 he opened the XXI Oecumenical Council at Vatican City.

63. 1978 AD

Pope Paul VI (1963-1978) presided over the Oecumenical Council, closing it in 1965 declaring its decrees Church doctrine. The mass and sacraments were to be conducted in the vernacular and a considerable number of 'saints' deposed. In 1968 he condemned artificial measures of birth control and in 1969 fought the Italian divorce law. Once more it seemed the Church's internal logic was better than its perception of the world outside it – Canute had reappeared! However, especially in the non-Catholic Western Christian world a sort of revival was building of a basically non-establishment variety. The Jesus Freaks, Children of God, etc. and the Pentecostal Movement in general, rock operas *Godspell* and *Jesus Christ Superstar et al.* mirror an emotional dissatisfaction with the intellectualism of the Christian establishment and an urge to get 'high' without drugs. The movement may also have reflected disaffection with the Marxist Faith Answer, as its social perfective and 'scientific' economic claims become increasingly absurd.

64. 1978 AD

Pope John Paul II (1978-), Polish and thoroughly acquainted with the actual functioning of the Marxist Faith Answer, proved a brilliant publicist of the papacy. Although in reality a thorough-going conservative in his opposition to artificial birth-control, divorce, abortion, marriage of priests, ordaining of women and many other changes, his personal charm and absolute dedication helped him to overcome mounting criticism from reformists. He too rode, to some extent, a mini-Christian revival – hence the small recovery in the chart for the last two Popes.

65. 1995 AD

The removal of the Berlin Wall, the collapse of Marxist governments in Europe and the Soviet Union, and the parody of Marxism – 'get rich quick' – in China, deprived the Papacy of its 20th-century sparring partner. Its *raison d'etre* as a shelter against the 'storm' of dialectical malism was gone. So, paradoaterixically, organized, traditional Christianity has not benefitted from the end of its enemy. It has actually **become weaker through no longer having to be strong.**

Pope John Paul II, preaching his messianic Catholic conservatism despite ailing health, tended to be welcomed as a super star rather than the bearer of vital tidings. The failure of the Church to come to terms with important matters such as birth control, became recognized as an increasingly erroneous stance. In the last decade of the 20th Century, the political and intellectual collapse of Marxism removed the importance of the Pope's opposition to it.

For that reason the graph begins to head downward toward the end of the 'Polish Papacy'.

Conclusion

Christianity arose out of a reaction to the materialism of the Roman Empire and the presence of the Roman occupying force in Palestine. The Jewish collaborationists provided Jesus with a focal point for his attack; however, it is very likely that, without Paul the Apostle's brilliant construction and synthesis of Christian dogma and his internationalizing and organizing Christian messianism, Christianity would have been just another escape for disaffected Jews in the Roman Empire.

As ideas of the 'spirit' became more fashionable than those of 'flesh', intellectuals found their outlet first in Neoplatonism (Plotinus 204-270 AD) *et al.* and then Christianity. A system was constructed which subordinated science to revelation. As long as the Christian 'iron curtain' could keep out foreign ideas and the Church maintain an absolute control over all forms of education, the system held. But perhaps it was its sense of security, rightness and indisputable power which opened the chinks in its own armour. Through the crusading wars against the Moors, Syrian-Egyptian Moslems and finally their fellow-Christians in Constantinople, Christians discovered other peoples who had preserved far more of the Greco-Roman civilization than they. The period of influx of foreign ideas (to Western Christianity), rediscovery of an ancient non-Christian past, and the digestion of these cultural shocks occurred coincidentally with a sharp decline in the quality of the Popes, as well as external political difficulties. The papacy that began to appear after the 1409 debacle of the three Popes was primarily interested in the material, artistic and intellectual joys of the Renaissance version of the Greco-Roman world and so ignored reform and reformers. But even so, science, so long restrained by revelation, would have probably pushed Christianity back into the emotional and metaphysical corner from which it emerged. The 'best' of the Popes could only have bought a few more years of monolithic hegemony.

Present-day Christianity is more vigorous where it least attempts system-building and Augustinian-Thomian intellectual justification. Where it 'sticks to its last', staying away from inter-disciplinary pronouncements of a technical nature, and offers emotional excitement and ecstasy, it fills its coffers and its churches.

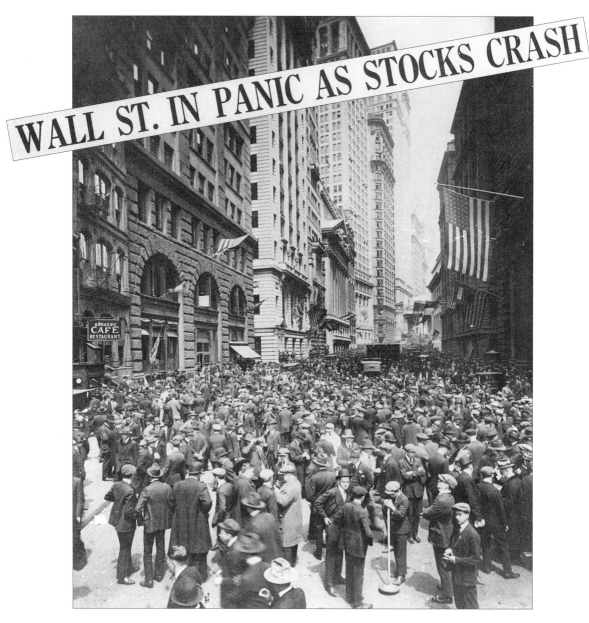

200 Black Monday, October 21, 1929. Marxism's crash came in 1991.

INDEX

fn=footnote, cp=chart point